SLIPKNOT

unmasked (again)

OMNIBUS PRESS

London · New York · Paris · Sydney · Copenhagen · Madrid · Tokyo

Copyright © 2003 Omnibus Press
(A Division of Music Sales Limited)

Cover & Book designed by Fresh Lemon.
Picture research by Joel McIver & Nikki Lloyd.

ISBN: 0.7119.9764.0
Order No: OP 49357

Exclusive Distributors
Music Sales Limited,
8/9 Frith Street, London W1D 3JB, UK.

Music Sales Corporation,
257 Park Avenue South, New York, NY 10010, USA.

Macmillan Distribution Services,
53 Park West Drive, Derrimut, Vic 3030, Australia.

To the Music Trade only:
Music Sales Limited,
8/9 Frith Street, London W1D 3JB, UK.

Photo credits:
Antler/Retna: 34; Craig Barritt/Retna: 10, 26, 64; Paul Booth: 14;
Josh Brainard (www.ox30.com): 13; Grant Davis/Retna: 33, 48, 9x colour;
Yo-Yo Feldman: 15, 16, 22; Martyn Goodacre/Retna: 47, 52, 85, 1x colour;
Mick Hutson/Redferns: 74, 77; Ixo/Avantis/Rex: 86;
Dennis Kleiman/Retna: 66/67, 1x colour; Mike Lawyer: 18, 20, 1x colour;
Pascal Leopold/Rex: 100; John McMurtrie/Retna: 94; Xavier Popy/Rex: 99;
Nicky J. Sims/Redferns: 40, 60; Nick Stevens/Retna: 6, 104, 109;
Jeremy Sutton/Rex: 97; David Titlow/Camera Press: 3
LFI: f&b cover, inside f&b cover, 9, 31, 37, 39, 43, 44, 55, 56, 61,
63, 71, 73, 81, 82, 91, 7x colour.

Printed by Page Bros. Limited, Norwich, Norfolk, UK.

A catalogue record for this book is available from the British Library.

Visit Omnibus Press on the web at www.omnibuspress.com

OMNIBUS PRESS PRESENTS THE STORY OF

SlipKnot

unmasked (again)

A BIOGRAPHY BY JOEL McIVER

PAGE 08

PAGE 11

PAGE 19

PAGE 27

PAGE 35

PAGE 41

PAGE 49

INTRODUCTION &
ACKNOWLEDGEMENTS

1 **2** **3** **4** **5** **6**

BEFORE 1995

1995 – 1996

1996

1996 – 1997

1997

1997 – 1998

PAGE 57

7

1 9 9 8 — 1 9 9 9

1 9 9 8 — 1 9 9 9

PAGE 65

8

1 9 9 9

1 9 9 9

PAGE 75

9

2 0 0 0

1 9 9 9 — 2 0 0 0

PAGE 87

10

2 0 0 1

2 0 0 0 — 2 0 0 1

PAGE 95

11

2 0 0 2

2 0 0 1 — 2 0 0 2

PAGE 105

12

B E Y O N D

2 0 0 3 & B E Y O N D

PAGE 111

D I S C O G R A P H Y

COREY TAYLOR

PERSONNEL	95	EVENTS

January 1995: Shawn Crahan, Anders Colselfni, Paul Gray, Donnie Steele and Kun Nong start rehearsals. **February**: Kun Nong leaves. **May**: Joey Jordison joins. **September**: Josh Brainard joins.

Spring and Summer 1995: Band forms and rehearses in Anders Colsefnis basement. **November**: band plays gig at Crowbar under name Meld. **December**: band visits SR Audio and Sean McMahon comes to practice. Band begin recording.

96

January 1996: Donnie leaves. Craig Jones joins.

April: Mick Thompson joins.

Spring 1996: Slipknot name chosen. Gigs at Safari Club. Mixdown of MFKR album.

October: MFKR album launch.

97

May 1997: Corey Taylor joins.

June: Anders leaves.

September: Greg 'Cuddles' Welts joins.

Summer 1997: Dotfest; vocalist shuffle.

Autumn: Ross Robinson contacted by Sophia John.

December: Robinson visites Slipknot.

98

June 1998: Greg leaves.

August: Chris Fehn leaves.

October: Sid Wilson joins.

May 1998: Slipknot plays EATM festival in Las Vegas.

July: Slipknot signs deal with Roadrunner.

December: Slipknot enters Indigo Ranch to record debut album.

99

January 1999: Josh Brainard leaves.

March: James Root joins.

June 1999: Slipknot album released.

Summer: Ozzfest.

Autumn: Livin La Vida Loco tour of USA and Canada.

00

November 2000: The Rejects and Joey Jordison rehearse and play live in Des Moines

Spring and Summer 2000: World tour.

01

January 2001: Band return to studio for third album.

February: Grammy nomination.

July: Iowa released

Winter: World tour

02

Spring 2002: Stone Sour reform with James Root and Corey Taylor and sign to Roadrunner.

The Rejects change their name to the Murderdolls and also sign to Roadrunner.

August 2002: Stone Sour and Beyond The Valley Of the Murderdolls albums released

03

Summer 2003: Stone Sour and Murderdolls tour together

Slipknot in studio recording next album, to be released in early 2004

INTRODUCTION & ACKNOWLEDGEMENTS

This is the story of Slipknot – a band that has shocked, fascinated and enthralled rock and metal fans like few others. This group of somewhat unusual individuals has spent the last five years spreading their particular message – composed of two parts bile and unbalanced invective to one part surprising intelligence and sensitivity – and being as much reviled as worshipped for their efforts. Their understanding of the needs and appetites of their audience is far-reaching, their commitment is deeply impressive and their musicianship and songwriting skills are head and shoulders above many of their contemporaries.

But why should we care, I hear you ask? It's only a band.

It's a fair question. Slipknot's detractors claim that the band relies on puerile shock tactics to retain an audience; that when you strip away the lurid exterior of the band, you're left with some pretty basic rock; and that it's all been done before – many, many times before. If it's unpredictable heavy metal with influences lifted from disparate musical genres that you're after, you only have to look back a few years to see it. The Nineties saw heavily made-up acts such as Marilyn Manson and Coal Chamber strike it lucky; the Eighties were the province of quirk-metallers Faith No More; and the Seventies, of course, were every pansticked glam-rocker's heyday, from Bowie and Bolan at the posh end right through to Alice Cooper and Kiss down in the undergrowth.

All this is true, as far as it goes. But it's far from being the whole truth. Slipknot differ from the thousands of other rock and metal bands which make up the popular music scene of today in two vital ways.

Firstly, like all zeitgeist-defining bands (think back to the uncouth sneer of The Rolling Stones, the vitriolic misanthropy of The Sex Pistols, the calculated hostility of Ice-T) Slipknot are angry with the world they live in. Exacerbated by the unremitting dullness of their immediate environment, this anger informs and drives their work, leading to an expression so powerful that no-one with an open mind can mistake their message. There's no faking or posturing here. They really mean it.

Secondly, yes – they *are* highly visual. They wear masks. Their on-stage antics are so driven as to be hypnotic, and at times the anarchy that surrounds them can be pretty scary. But underneath this, when you look under the surface – and in this book I believe I have, for the first time ever – there are real people with real views and a highly accurate take on their environment. They don't go home after a show, take off their masks and settle down with a cup of tea, but they don't live a consciously 'rock star' life, either. What they have is substance – and that's sorely lacking in bands of any kind nowadays.

That's why you should care.

As this book is the first of many which I'm sure will be published about Slipknot, accurate information about them is scarce. This meant that my research has turned up a mountain of data which hasn't been publicised before. It would have been an impossible task without the help of the following people.

First of all, my sincere thanks go to Kyle Munson, music critic with the *Des Moines Register*. All material reproduced from the *Register* is done so with its publisher's kind permission.

Mike Lawyer, the owner of SR Audio, the recording studio that first launched Slipknot into the world, was also very unselfish with his time and unafraid to tell the truth on one

Brown Publishing for his kind permission to reproduce material from *Viz* magazine, Adrian Pertout for permission to use extracts from his work and Jeff Seybert for his balanced analysis of the city of Des Moines. Thanks too to the visitors to the alt.music.slipknot newsgroup, whose posts were extremely useful.

Thanks, of course, to Slipknot themselves,

or two occasions when an airbrushed version of it might have sufficed. Thanks also to the producer Sean McMahon, who passed a message to Shawn Crahan on my behalf.

The first Slipknot singer Anders Colsefni and the guitarist Josh Brainard were happy to give me an insight into life inside the band from a perspective that only they have. I wish them the best of luck with their new bands Painface and Undone.

Thanks to Michelle Kerr at Roadrunner in the UK for all the superb albums, Kas Mercer at Mercenary PR for setting up an interview with Ross Robinson and all my colleagues at *Record Collector* for tolerating my ever-growing obsession with Slipknot over the past year.

Many thanks to Edward Axon at John

for providing such a deeply satisfying noise. They didn't want to be involved in this book for their own reasons, but nonetheless I wish them the best of luck with their career and hope they stick around to annoy, provoke and thrill us for many years to come. I hope they enjoy reading my interpretation of their story – it's a bizarre tale, all right.

My gratitude goes out as always to my friends and family, who carefully listened to my explanation of Slipknot and their role in modern metal before nodding wisely and saying, "How interesting. Who is it again?"

Finally, thanks to Emma, who makes it all worthwhile.

Joel McIver, February 2001
Email: joel@joelmciver.co.uk

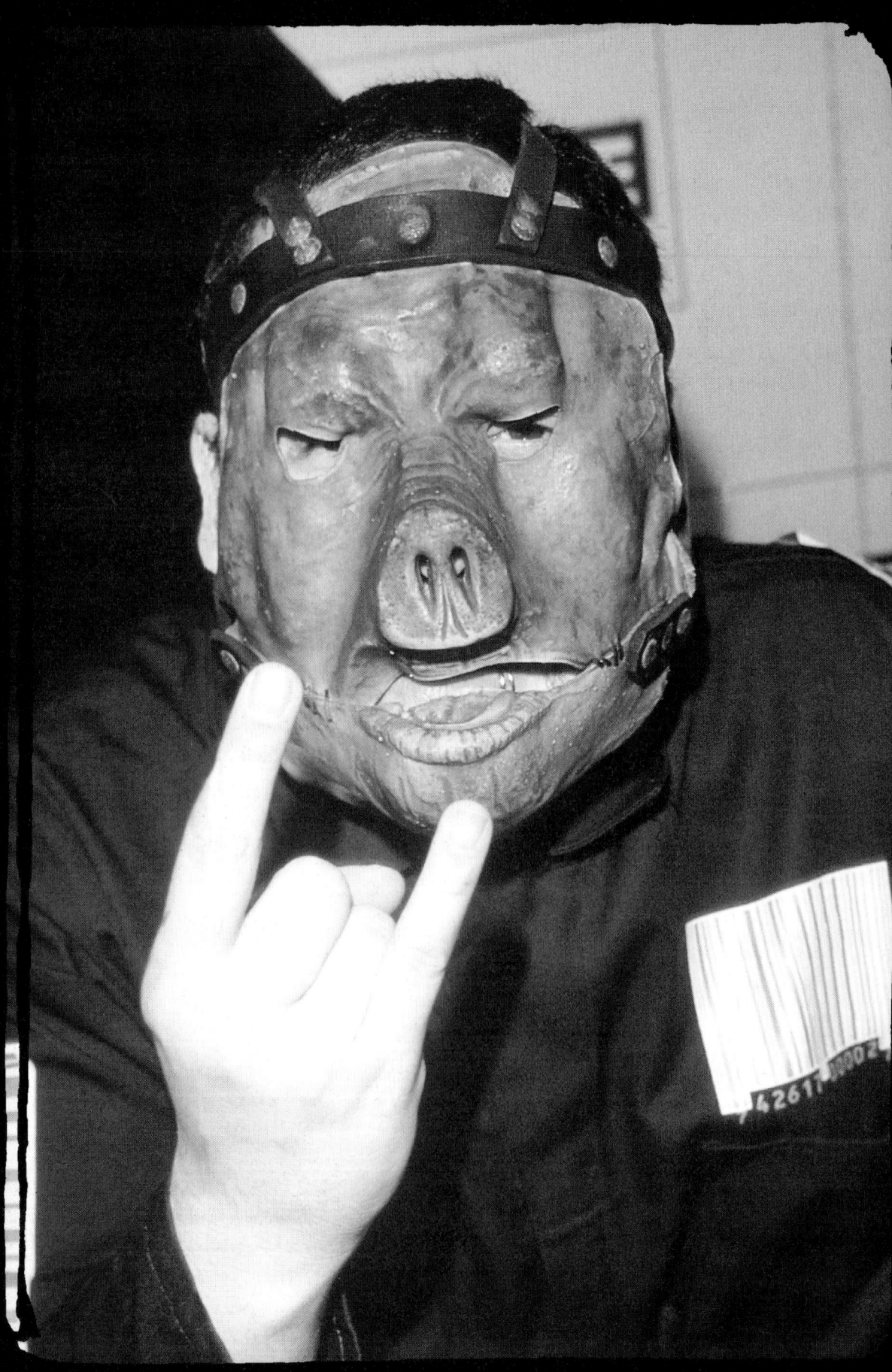

CHAPTER ONE

BEFORE 1995

"I come from Des Moines. Somebody had to."

BILL BRYSON, THE LOST CONTINENT

If there was ever a town deserving of the label "the middle of nowhere", Des Moines is it.

You'll find it approximately due west of Chicago, just south of the midpoint of Iowa. It's the state's capital city – and its biggest - and is also the seat of Polk County. Physically, it's unremarkable; the Des Moines and Raccoon rivers meet nearby; it's the home of Drake University, founded in 1881; and, as you might expect, it specialises in the administration, processing and distribution of Iowa's enormous corn trade. Like many other cities, it's also home to the automotive industry and others such as food and printing.

About 90% of Des Moines' citizens are white, with the remainder largely taken up by its black and Hispanic communities as well as native Americans and Asians. The total number of residents – a little under 200,000 – has fluctuated only by an estimated 1% over the last two decades, which would seem to indicate a city in comfortable stasis if not in a boom period. It's a quiet, relaxed town, according to popular opinion. More than this, though – it's a conservative town. There's unlikely to be a thriving underground culture, whether of music, drugs, crime or otherwise. Life-changing events (in the musical field, at any rate) don't come along very often – but when they do, they make a hell of an impact. An infamous example was the banning of C. W. McCall's January 1976 'Convoy' single by a leading Des Moines radio station. The reason? Because the programmers believed (allegedly, m'lud) that the song incited truck drivers to break speed limits. As an illumination of the cultural stance of the city's establishment figures, this will do nicely. But worse was to come.

In late 1982, Des Moines was scheduled for a visit by one of the godfathers of heavy metal, Ozzy Osbourne, sometime singer with the British metal behemoths Black Sabbath and a hell-raiser of almost mythical fame.

The show was notable for an incident that occurred towards the end of the set when a member of the audience threw a live bat onto the stage. The singer, assuming it to be made of rubber, picked it up and bit off its head. Although he realised his error instants later and spat out the offending mouthful, he was rushed immediately to the nearest hospital, where he had his stomach pumped and more painfully, endured a series of precautionary anti-rabies injections.

The effect of this show on the metal fans of Des Moines was electrifying. Among those who weren't at the concert, but wished he could have been when he came across radio

which he named Heads On The Wall. The line-up included an Asian teenager named Kun Nong – an excellent guitarist by all accounts – and a bass player named Doug, who also handled vocals. Proficient by high-school standards, the band exceeded most teenage groups' ambitions by playing at venues all over Iowa. Musically, their funk-metal and old-school thrash influences were clear; their gigs included Eighties hits by The Red Hot Chili Peppers (whose early albums possessed a grittier, funkier edge than their later, more polished work) and went as far as covering songs by quirky, unclassifiable acts such as Primus and Jane's Addiction.

"I'd say we were all hyperactive, and depressed, and just fucking always in trouble – you know, just doing our thing" SHAWN CRAHAN

and newspaper reports of the bat's untimely demise, was a 12-year-old schoolkid by the name of Shawn Crahan. Born in September 1969 to real estate developers, Crahan was obsessed with exploring the city's labyrinthine storm drains – dark, undisturbed tunnels big enough for an adult to walk through – and playing the drums. His earliest musical heroes were Kiss: the very first album he had ever bought was *Dynasty*, and it was Peter Criss who first inspired him to become a drummer. When asked in 1999 by the Seattlesquare.com webzine what the future members of Slipknot were like as children, Shawn said, "I'd say we were all hyperactive, and depressed, and just fucking always in trouble - you know, just doing our thing. I think we were all nutty little kids, and I think maybe some of us were really quiet and just looking out from the inside."

By the time he was 15, Shawn had honed his drumming skills enough to form a band at Des Moines' Hoover High School,

Along with Heads On The Wall, another successful local band was the unusually named Vexx, a tougher, more accomplished act than Heads whose music was technical, complex death metal. To the untrained ear, there may not *be* much difference between thrash and death metal, but where thrash can be fairly tinny, with wailed or barked vocals, death metal is a deeper, more brutal sound, with an intensity found in no other musical genre and featuring roared, bellowed or vomited vocals. This doesn't mean it's all about aggression, though, or simple to play; to produce it to any competent degree, players of every instrument must master their art absolutely, as it's often unpredictable and usually precise. In short, it can be hard work for both listener and performer – but when it's done well (Morbid Angel, Deicide, Nile) it is metal at its very best.

Vexx – which later went under the slightly ridiculous name of Inveigh Catharsis - produced hard-hitting, inventive death

metal: its drummer was the thick-set Anders Colsefni, an intimidating figure with a Mohican haircut. Colsefni had developed a very aggressive, uncompromising percussion technique, which became a high point of Vexx shows. The bassist was Paul Gray, a superb player who had mastered the guitar before moving to bass. Originally from Los Angeles, Paul had recently wound up in Des Moines and – perhaps wanting to recapture the positive, do-it-all vibe of California – had thrown himself into the band with gusto. On guitar was Josh Brainard, another accomplished player who was initially from New Mexico and had moved several times before his teens, finally ending up in Des Moines after a move from the nearby town of Waterloo.

Vocals were initially handled by Josh, whose skills as a multi-tasking frontman were temporarily put on hold in around 1990 when Anders started to sing: Colsefni had a powerful baritone voice – rather like that of Soulfly's Max Cavalera or Testament's Chuck Billy – which suited the death metal style perfectly. Vexx spent some years playing low-key gigs with a certain degree of success; however, on looking back, Colsefni now describes it as "pointlessly technical", claiming that the band would play for the sake of complexity alone, with perhaps up to 20 chord changes in the space of a single three-minute song. Unsurprisingly, they never recorded.

Josh Brainard later hooked up with another guitarist called Joey Jordison, who had put together a band called Modifidious in 1992 with another six-stringer called Craig Jones. The three swapped bass and guitar duties, while Brainard also handled vocals. The music they played was straight-ahead thrash metal, something like the squeaky-clean speed of Anthrax – not as demanding as the heavier material of Vexx, but light-years ahead of the rather eccentric funk-rock of Heads On The Wall. Modifidious had the dubious distinction of being labelled "Monkey Fungus Dick" and

BEHIND THE (BONDAGE) MASK: JOSH BRAINARD

other 'humorous' nicknames by visiting musicians; however, Jordison (who had invented the name as a meaningless nonsense word) saw the funny side. The high point in Modifidious' career was definitely a Des Moines support slot with the goth-metallers Type O Negative in 1995.

To this day, however, several different spellings exist for the name – Motifidious, Modividious and so on. It's indicative of Joey's somewhat skewed sense of humour that one of his early bands was labelled with a word that no-one could spell. He remains a slightly eccentric but likeable spokesman for Slipknot, and one of its most talented members. After studying the guitar – he also plays six-string in a hardcore punk band called The Rejects – he picked up the drums. A phenomenal player, his skills have been honed by over 15 years of study, aided by his devotion to the warp-speed techniques of black metal, which demands absolute precision and stamina from those who play it.

Perhaps the most extreme of the early- to mid-Nineties Des Moines metal bands that

come into the Slipknot story was the superbly named Anal Blast. This band was formed partly as a joke, partly as a publicity stunt and partly as a serious grindcore outfit by Jordison, Vexx's Paul Gray, a guitarist by the name of Donnie Steele and a concert promoter called Don Decker, an enormously obese singer who was (and still is) involved in setting up metal shows and festivals throughout the Midwestern states. Jordison, Steele and Gray would play merrily along, while Decker indulged in such onstage antics as reaching into the seat of his trousers, pulling out a tampon which had been inserted in his rectum and throwing it into the crowd. Occasionally, if this failed to elicit the desired reaction, Decker would step offstage, return with a toilet bowl and, as they say, "lay a carpet".

Despite these shock tactics, the band appears to have been more than just a joke act; in fact, Anal Blast is the only band mentioned here to still exist today, along with The Rejects. An album, *Vaginal Vempire*, has been on sale for some time; Jordison has claimed that he and Paul wrote much or all of the material on it. Its cover is a pornographic spoof of the *Vempire: Or Dark Fairyales In Phallustein* album by the successful British black metal band Cradle Of Filth, and indeed Decker describes his band as "sick brutal porno grindcore".

As talented – or not – as these bands all were, the local Des Moines music scene in the mid-Nineties was in thrall to one act only: an alternative rock/metal outfit named Stone Sour, which is also the name (coincidentally or otherwise) of a popular American cocktail. Their singer, Corey Taylor, earned a living by working in a porn shop.

To a certain extent in Stone Sour – but more notably in his later band – Corey would reveal his inner demons through the lyrics he wrote and the exertions of his stage act. In his teens he had both sides of his neck tattooed; one side with the Chinese symbol for 'death', reproduced from the Kanji

NOW THAT'S GOT TO HURT...
COREY TAYLOR'S UNCOMPROMISING BODY ART

alphabet, and the other with the character for 'father'. This, it would appear, lies at the root of much of the anger in his songs: Taylor never knew his father, who abandoned his mother even before Corey's birth. He once said in an interview that between the ages of four and eleven, he had lived in 25 different states. Originally trained as a drummer, he moved to vocals after hearing the Nirvana song 'Bleach', in which the late Kurt Cobain indicated his dissatisfaction with the world in no uncertain terms.

Despite the local successes of Stone Sour, Corey later described their music as "half originals, half cheesy Top 40 crap" – he evidently regards the band now as a stepping-stone towards Slipknot, and perhaps this can be said of all the early bands mentioned here: Jordison has referred to Slipknot as a "supergroup" in various interviews. This is not to say that these other acts were incompetent or unprofessional; for example, a prominent local outfit at the time was Atomic Opera, who Anders Colsefni has described as "the band that set the standard for all Iowan metal bands at the time". Their guitarist, James Root, was a gifted

player whose onstage presence was impressive.

The last – and most incestuous, as it were – of the Des Moines bands was another death metal outfit called Body Pit. Anders Colsefni describes it as "very heavy death metal. Very intricate - too intricate. Eight-minute long songs, with 25 different riffs in each song. Nuts. Heavy, but nuts." Before departing for Los Angeles, Paul Gray contributed heavily to their songs; the band also featured Colsefni on drums and two brutal guitarists, Mick Thompson and Donnie Steele. Mick is a powerful, intimidating figure, on and off stage, though his uncompromising appearance belies a serious musical talent – for many years he gave guitar lessons at the somewhat winsomely named Ye Olde Guitar Shop on 70th Street.

Donnie Steele was also looking for a more serious band, and had got to know Shawn Crahan and Anders Colsefni through the spaghetti-junction-like local metal scene. The first move towards the formation of the band we know now as Slipknot took place in early 1995, when Colsefni, Crahan, Steele and Heads On The Wall's Kun Nong met at Anders' house with the vague aim of jamming together. Although they had grown up playing in different bands, Crahan and Colsefni had been friends since the early Nineties when they had attended metal gigs together: the pair first discussed a music project after Shawn called Anders and recruited him for a photo shoot. "They wanted a scary-looking person," recalls Colsefni today. "The shoot was for a paper company, who were using some kind of 'intolerance' theme for their advertising. I had a Mohawk haircut and they thought I looked right for the photo. I got to put my arms round an intolerant-looking girl. It was fun."

The two men (Anders: "Me and Shawn looked just alike – both with Mohawks that we tied back in pony-tails, both kinda mean-looking") had also developed a mutual interest in the role-playing game, *Rage: The Apocalypse*, a tougher, bloodier extension of the many RPGs that had flooded the market since the late-Seventies/early-Eighties success of *Dungeons & Dragons*. Issued by the White Wolf company, *Rage*'s central theme was the conflict of a werewolf race, the Garou, with the Wyrm, an evil tribe.

ANDERS COLSEFNI

According to Colsefni, the game was a way of life: "The attraction was being able to play a different person, to be able to do something different. This was the founding of Slipknot – that was it, right there."

After working on some welding at Shawn's garage in the winter of 1994 to 1995, the two began talking about putting a band together. This wasn't the first time

played in his basement. This became their regular meeting place for the next two years.

The next – and pivotal – decision was to invite Joey Jordison to join, in the early summer. The horrible Anal Blast was only sporadically active, and Modifidious was also a part-time project, so Jordison was happy to accept. This left both Anders and Shawn free to do other things onstage: Colsefni became

Crahan and Colsefni had tried to form a band; they had attempted to recruit musicians before, but the project had fallen apart before it began after Shawn became temporarily involved in his father's real estate business. This time, however, the situation was serious: both men were tired of being in limited, unprofessional bands and agreed to make a no-holds-barred attempt to form a serious group of musicians.

Anders called Paul Gray, who had recently moved to California, and after some patient persuasion, Gray agreed to return. With the bassist installed, the musicians met two or three times a week at Colsefni's house, where they

the group's voice, while Crahan took over a second set of percussion. Joey didn't regret his decision: in fact he later said, "When I first came into the band I was like – I have to be either in this band or I have to destroy it because it's so good."

The band's sound was still relatively unsophisticated at this stage: Kun Nong had quit after a few sessions ("Phenomenal, crazy guitar player – but not a *metal* guitar player" says Anders) and Donnie's powerful playing, complemented by Paul and Joey, had become the focus of the music. He was a fan of soul and jazz as well as metal, a fact which made itself clear in one of the early songs,

'Confessions', which was more or less a pop workout along the lines of much early white funk – except, of course, for Anders' vocals, which were melodic but fairly guttural. However, the band agreed that, while progress was definitely being made, another guitarist was needed to fill out the sound. Joey immediately suggested the Modifidious guitarist Josh Brainard. Josh remembers, "Joey told them I could play, I could sing and I had stage presence. So they called me up and asked me to go watch them rehearse."

Brainard duly attended a band practice and was impressed by the ability and commitment of the players. As he watched,

upstairs and the metal and rock at the bottom."

After some deliberation, they agreed to perform, but they still needed a name, and Josh suggested Meld. As one of the band's declared aims had been to mix any genres of music they liked, the name was adopted, though Josh was later humiliated to discover that a 'meld' is also a move in a card game: "It was like calling ourselves Blackjack or Poker – totally tacky!" he says now.

And so, on December 4, the band made its live debut. "We weren't technically ready to play," says Anders. "But it was a good gig. We didn't have costumes or anything,

"The attraction was being able to play a different person, to be able to do something different. This was the founding of Slipknot – that was it, right there." ANDERS COLSEFNI

Shawn asked him if he would like to bring a guitar to the next session. Josh was only too pleased to oblige and meshed rapidly with the other players: "Donnie already had the riffs done," he remembers. "I just learned them and played my own contributions over the top." He's being over-modest – his role in the early Slipknot songwriting was significant – but what's certain is that he was accepted into the band with little hesitation.

Josh joined the band in September 1995. Within a month the musicians had assembled a set's worth of songs, though the lack of a suitable venue meant that no great efforts were made to secure a live date. Then a friend asked them to perform at a benefit concert in aid of a local charity at a club called the Crowbar, a venue which Josh remembers as "a multi-level place with a hip-hop place in the middle, a country place

but we freaked the hell out of everybody." He also later said that a Slipknot performance is "a primal feeling. I'm transformed into an animal, and that's the reason we wear what we do on stage." The set was short and brutal, including the songs 'Slipknot', 'Tattered And Torn', 'Rights And Rage', 'Some Feel', 'Only One' and a soon-to-be-dropped thrash metal effort called 'Part Of Me', which featured a rap from Josh. 'Confessions', always a difficult song to perform live, wasn't attempted. The band managed to disguise its inexperience through sheer punkish exuberance.

It was the last chance a live audience ever had to see the band fully unmasked. Although it was an uncertain performance, with the songs played in their rawest form, if you were there, you witnessed a milestone in modern music.

CHAPTER TWO

1995–1996

As 1995 drew to a close, the six-piece band continued to rehearse at Anders Colsefni's house. The issue of a name had become more pressing: Josh had unearthed the card-sharp's definition of the word 'meld' and they settled on the title of the opening song of their Crowbar set for a new name – perhaps they wouldn't have done so, had they known how many journalists would later plague them for a meaning in their choice of Slipknot.

"We don't actually think about what a 'slipknot' is," said Joey much later. Over the years, fans and press have come up with all kinds of possible interpretations of the word – after all, it can imply choking, gagging or hanging (with all the murder and S&M connotations you might expect) or simply claustrophobia and unease.

When you have six motivated musicians in a band, things move rapidly, and at the very end of the year Shawn, Joey and Josh visited a local recording studio, SR Audio, located in the Des Moines suburb of Urbandale, to record an album. The studio owner, a man experienced in the ways of the music business, was Mike Lawyer, who took the musicians around the building and arranged for one of his producers, Sean McMahon, to visit the newly-christened Slipknot at a practice session. Mike takes up the story:

"Sean went to see them at a rehearsal. He came in the next day and his eyes were wide open – and he said, 'Last night I saw the most original band I have *ever* seen in the Midwest'. And McMahon worked for ten years in the Bay area in San Francisco, he worked at Memphis, he worked at St Louis, he's worked everywhere – and he said, there's something here."

McMahon later described himself as "floored" by Slipknot. Anders, who made a point at the time of rehearsing in a natty wolf-skin loincloth, had made an enormous impression on the producer. When asked what had struck McMahon, Lawyer explains: "It was just how *different* they were. First of all they were great musicians: they didn't sound like anything anybody else was doing, especially not in Des Moines, Iowa! The closest thing they might have sounded

19

PRODUCER SEAN McMAHON AND COREY TAYLOR

like at that time might have been Sepultura. A little bit. And the way they merged all these styles – jazz, disco, whatever – really impressed him."

Anders – who remembers Sean McMahon as "very professional, very prim and proper" – explains the producer's reaction as follows: "The diversity and the technicality of Slipknot astounded him, and the fact that we had so many layers in the music. He was pleased because we were a good band, and because it was going to be a challenge like he'd never had before. This was in 1995, remember – we had only played one gig, and we hadn't even planned to play that. But we still impressed him."

that Slipknot paints in the interviews they do makes it sound like the whole reason they are who they are, is because Des Moines is so terrible. But, in all honesty, I wouldn't choose to live here if it was so terrible. If you're looking for an exciting, LA-style lifestyle, it's not that. But it's definitely not a hole in the bottom of a pit like it's portrayed nowadays."

The consequences of Sean McMahon's meeting with Slipknot were twofold. Firstly, the band were booked into the studio in December to record a debut album. They would fund this themselves and, as they were mostly supporting themselves with day jobs, the sessions would take place at night-time. Secondly – and perhaps more significantly –

"One of the goals I set myself ten years ago was to see if we could be a part of getting a band to break out of Iowa. And Slipknot has accomplished that goal." MIKE LAWYER

One explanation for his reaction, of course, is that Des Moines was not known for the innovation or visual imagery of its bands. As Lawyer points out, "In my lifetime – and I'm 39 years old – there have only been three groups from Iowa that have been signed to what would be considered major record deals. One was The Jan Park Band, a pop band back in the late Seventies, the second was The Hawks, who were on CBS and lasted two albums, and the other is Slipknot." He adds (with a certain degree of pride, and who can blame him?), "One of the goals I set myself ten years ago was to see if we could be a part of getting a band to break out of Iowa. And Slipknot has accomplished that goal."

This is not to say that Des Moines is entirely without artistic or other cultural activity. He laughs as he says, "The picture

McMahon went on to sign a production deal with Slipknot, in which he agreed that after producing the album, he would work with the band towards a record deal in return for a share in any future profits.

Rock and metal was in an uncertain state at the time of Slipknot's formation. Both McMahon and Lawyer were experts when it came to analysing the music of the day, and both were blown away by the Slipknot attack – but who were their contemporaries? Take a look at Slipknot's influences. The most obvious of these is Korn. Perhaps the first of many bands to be labelled – positively or otherwise – with tags such as "emo-core", "emo-metal" or the most common, "nu-metal", Korn were and remain a powerful, uncompromising band from the isolated community of Bakersfield in California. Like Slipknot, they suffered initially from a

great deal of small-town resentment and, again like Slipknot, chose to exorcise this through the brutality of their music.

Nu-metal nowadays – and whether they like it or not, Slipknot are usually labelled with this term, along with acts such as Deftones, Amen and Incubus – has become an accepted genre of its own. Back in 1995, the original pioneers of the style, Rage Against The Machine, had issued their groundbreaking first album to widespread acclaim – but are now on hold since the

Metal had spent the latter half of the Nineties rediscovering itself – and it was in this frame of mind that McMahon welcomed Slipknot to SR Audio one evening in late December, 1995, to lay down tracks for the first album, the bleakly-titled *Mate. Feed. Kill. Repeat.* Anders later explained the title as a representation of the cycle of life: "You mate to reproduce, feed to survive, kill the opposition – and then the cycle repeats itself." Anders and Josh recall the sessions as confused, chaotic and even anarchic, but

STUDIO OWNER MIKE LAWYER AT SR AUDIO

departure of the outspoken singer Zack de la Rocha. Mention must be made once again of Sepultura, who perhaps epitomise the development of nu-metal more than most. Founder member Max Cavalera left the band in 1997 to form a new band, the very successful Soulfly – and the press have now labelled him "the godfather of nu-metal".

Finally, the band which many credit with bringing extreme metal to the masses – Metallica – is now nothing less than a mainstream rock band. At the time of Slipknot's first emergence, they were still known as a metal band – but their *Load* and *Reload* albums of 1996 and 1998 were so much more lightweight than their previous work that much of their original audience has more or less abandoned them.

one thing is for sure – they were extremely productive. They must have been, since the contributions of six players over eight tracks were recorded in a mere seventy-two hours. The mix-down was a different story, however: over three months were required to produce a final mix with which all the band members were happy.

Mike Lawyer recalls the very first session: "Here's a story that's never been told. The studio's located in an industrial area, and so we share a building that has other offices around it, even though we're heavily soundproofed. I drove into the parking lot the next morning after Slipknot had had their very first session there the night before – and they had decorated half of a whole parking lot with chalk outline drawings,

like of dead bodies, like police outlines. Yet they had added things like huge penises and things to the outlines. All over the parking lot! I remember I said, this is going to be interesting... The neighbours never complained. Luckily the chalk washed off when it rained a few days later."

incomprehensible signature: "Joey's a multi-talented little prick," says Anders affectionately. "When we were recording *Mate. Feed. Kill. Repeat* he would scribble little dookie kid's pictures and make 'em look like little monsters and just leave them laying around and he'd sign it Corn Wallace."

ANDERS ONSTAGE - NOTE WOLFSKIN LOINCLOTH

Josh Brainard remembers this incident with great glee. "We were just letting off some steam, we'd been working for six or eight hours and we just wanted to do something else. We had a lot of good times in there."

Anders remembers that Sean McMahon would sometimes be so affected by the band's incessant drive that he would lie flat on his back on the studio floor, trying to regain his composure. Slipknot would come into the studio and decorate it bizarrely in order to inspire themselves – Joey in particular had a habit of leaving scrawled drawings of spiky-haired, sharp-toothed stick figures around the studio, each signed with an

It seems there were a few bizarre moments to treasure, including the recording of the final track on the album – the 10-minute 'Killers Are Quiet' – in a single take. One of the samples on this song is the sound of Anders tearing electrical tape off Shawn Crahan's face. The experience was so intense (particularly for Crahan – he punched Anders on the arm) that Colsefni decided there and then to wear the same kind of tape on his face onstage. He also recalls an argument with Joey, who once became so incensed that he ran out of the studio, screaming "I quit!" Travelling to the studio was also difficult: at one point the band had to negotiate three feet of snow to get there – this all took

place in December, in the middle of the fierce Midwestern winter.

Mike Lawyer has an explanation for Slipknot's special brand of insanity: "Because Slipknot are so anti-drink and anti-drugs – or at least because those things aren't what spurs their creativity – they really just thrived on their aggression."

Slipknot's public stance is not anti-drink and drugs, but they've made it clear that they choose not to partake. This ties in with the rise in popularity of the 'straightedge' lifestyle among young Americans, particularly hardcore punk and metal fans. Followers of this credo avoid all drugs, including alcohol and caffeine, are vegetarian or vegan and take pride in maintaining their physical health. Unsurprisingly, they're often the most committed headbangers at gigs, with the most concentrated energy and aggression.

But, like everyone else, Slipknot get annoyed with the world, and with no recourse to chemically-enhanced tranquility, the songs they write and the shows they perform are the outlet for this anger. Their need to react to the sterility of Des Moines gave added impetus to the vitriol and power of many Slipknot songs – and on this, their first album, that anger would have been at its rawest. Asked if he has fond memories of the *MFKR* sessions, Anders laughs and replies: "No, not really. I just remember the stress of always watching the clock – the time and the money is ticking away, you're trying to make everything perfect, and everything you think is going good actually isn't, so you've got to go back and redo stuff. When you hear yourself on tape without everybody else playing, you can hear all your errors."

Money was, of course, a perennial problem. Use of a professional studio and its staff doesn't come cheap. Anders estimates the total cost of recording and manufacturing 1,000 copies on CD as around $16,000, which Shawn paid with credit cards, while the others paid him back whenever they could. What's more, the band had hoped to complete the album within a budget of only

three to four thousand dollars: the collective drive to complete the album must have led Slipknot to the decision to finish what they had started despite the spiralling costs.

Josh Brainard also looks back on the *MFKR* sessions with one or two reservations. "To tell you the truth, sometimes I thought the studio was too sterile. That place was very clean, and I think the project would have turned out different if it had been recorded at a typical metal studio – you know, shit everywhere and the place 20 years old."

But despite these negative points, the musicians are agreed that the nine-track album – inexplicably described as an EP by some reviewers at the time – turned out to be a worthwhile recording. The opening track, 'Slipknot' developed into the well-known '[Sic]' on the second album, with rewritten lyrics and a brighter sound. This version is much slower and more threatening, and lyrically 'Slipknot' is pure *Rage*: Colsefni raves about the Pentex, Black Hand and Bonegnawers tribes ("Those wyrm-tainted bastard leeches!") with a throaty bellow worthy of the best death metal vocalists, and refers to the game's moves of "shifting into Crinos" and "stepping sideways to hide within the Umbra".

'Gently' is a more subtle, cerebral song, which opens gently but soon becomes a much heavier beast, with a mid-tempo set of riffs that pay homage to gloom-soaked industrial/gothic bands such as Type O Negative and Nine Inch Nails. There are even touches of Celtic Frost in the melody and Jordison's sporadic forays into thrash tempos late into the song. Colsefni sets a reflective mood with the line "Gently my mind escapes into the relaxing mode of pleasure /A pleasure that will take my mind off the reality of life" before yelling the repeated word "Shift!" – presumably another reference to the shape-changing strategies of *Rage*.

'Do Nothing/Bitch Slap' is the most complex song on the album, an astounding and sometimes incongruous mixture of death

metal, jazz noodling and even an extended disco workout which cuts in after two minutes. The atonal jazz guitar lines – probably from Donnie Steele, a self-confessed jazzbo – are a passable copy of the bebop maestro Django Reinhardt, all of which make the metal sections seem ultra-heavy in comparison. Lyrically, Anders indulges in some seriously vitriolic diatribe at some unidentified target: although the line "Chop down the big-wigs, shoot the televisions too / My mind boils in life as I've decided I'm through" is pretty gloomy. Anders later described the song as "a letter from a father to a son from whom he's been separated for about 17 years".

'Only One' was also reworked at a later point for the next album: like the later version, this mixture of rap-metal and screamed bile is a persuasive, precise song. "Pain – made to order!" growls Colsefni, before embarking on a nimble-tongued rap. Accompanied at first only by a rolling bass line, but later by some superb chicken-grease funk guitar, the choicest lyrics include near-gibberish such as "Sittin', slappin', scattin' on my back, tryin' to relax / Thinkin' about the facts of the crack runnin' through the pack" and a realistic vomiting sound. The repeated threat in the chorus ("Only one of us walks away!" repeated to murderous effect) remains one of the most intimidating lines Slipknot have ever written.

For those whose experience of the band is based on their second album, the early version of 'Tattered And Torn' may be a disappointment. It's a shorter, simpler and less sophisticated incarnation of Slipknot's well-known set highlight, retaining the ear-piercing lead guitar melody throughout, the burbling bass part and the multi-layered, anguished vocals, but it's not as cohesive or as memorable as the reworked version.

'Confessions' is a more fully-developed extension of the jazz and funk elements hinted at in 'Do Nothing'. There's no metal here: the song is nothing less than funk-pop, with hints at the proficiency of fusion.

It's a completely different side to Slipknot and not one that many fans will like. A sample line is "Trying to make amends for the Impergium / As Weaver and the Wyld and a bitch called the Wyrm". What's most surprising is the apparent ease with which the band slip into supper-club jazz mode.

'Some Feel' sees Slipknot back on form. Based around a deep, almost Morbid Angel riff, with a stop-start verse in an unusual time signature, it's in a style that fans of the latterday band will recognise. It's another heartfelt vampires-ahoy epic from Anders, and one of the heaviest songs here.

Perhaps the most unusual track for many is the closer, 'Killers Are Quiet', a lengthy, brooding, song full of bizarre samples taken from a variety of sources. As before, Anders avoids too many *Rage* references, although the song clearly revolves around the game's central themes: "Stepping sideways between worlds I shift / Killers are quiet when they are born with the gift". It's a slow-building song, with the obvious aim of creating an amorphous sound collage: never again would Slipknot be as experimental as this.

Shawn later referred to *Mate* as a 'demo' and stated: "That whole album didn't really have any structure." He has a point – it takes in so many styles that the listener is left with a mixture of impressions, and not really convinced that any of them is Slipknot's true direction. Still, as first albums go, it's a relatively accomplished effort. There was also a hidden track, 'Dogfish Rising', on which Joey played guitar and drums and Josh played bass. After a few minutes of silence following 'Killers Are Quiet', a melodic, hypnotic bass guitar chord sequence begins, accompanied by a deep background ambience like the noise of a distant aeroplane engine. This turns out to be the sub-bass timpani of Colsefni or Crahan, which adopts a tribal, rolling style. A more traditional metal riff starts up and the track goes on to be another slow, introspective composition in the vein of 'Gently'. It's a strange, disquieting song, and as it creeps to a close, you're reminded

of just what a weird set of psyches lie behind the album.

There are some noticeable variations in the sound across the record: some of the songs are more focused on the bottom end, with Gray's bass-lines and Jordison's kick drum more prominent, while others feature more of Colsefni's vocal or a meatier guitar sound. This is the result of the three different mixes which were made. Anders says, "The final mix and mastering wasn't completed until March or April – the CD makers were going to mix it and master it at the same time, but they kept screwing up the mastering because we had a couple of different mixes on the disk – Sean McMahon's and some that Joey helped mix. So Mike Lawyer did an in-studio master, it sounded good."

unwieldy, sharp-edged beast called Patiently Awaiting The Jigsaw Flesh. Crouching in the middle of the machine – which has been labelled "The Death Cage" by fans – and surrounded by girders and blade-like surfaces, is Joey wearing a white mask. Shawn has an artistic background – he's an admirer of the work of the French painter Cezanne, for example – and coupled with his training as a welder, the work is obviously his. "Every time we move it," he later said, "someone gets brutally cut." The inside tray of the CD's jewel case contains a picture of two other men, one of them Greg Welts, a friend of the band and an itinerant tattooist who had provided Anders with some body art, and David "Davo" Wilkins, another friend who worked at a piercing salon in Des Moines called The Axiom and who later booked

Shawn Crahan reached into his pocket and pulled out a dusty relic of his childhood... It was a clown mask.

When asked if he thinks *MFKR* turned out to be a good album, Josh – ever the professional – remarks: "Some of it – we were overly picky about certain things, I think it would have turned out better if we'd just let some of it go. When you have different mixes on a record, it makes it sound kind of disjointed from song to song." Colsefni, who thinks it *is* a good album, was relieved when Mike's master was completed: "One of the mixes – I can't remember which one – had way too much bass and kept farting-out the speakers."

After the three to four months of mixing-down and mastering was complete, all that remained was to select some artwork for the CD. The cover that was finally chosen was a dark green-tinted photograph of a metal sculpture designed by Crahan, an

bands to play at a local venue, the Safari Club on University Avenue.

One day in January 1996, after the recording of the album was complete but the mixing was still in progress, the band turned up to practice at Anders Colsefni's house as usual. While they were setting up their instruments – a lengthy, precise process for six musicians – Shawn Crahan reached into his pocket and pulled out a dusty relic of his childhood which he had found a couple of days before. He'd been moving boxes around his basement prior to moving house, and had come across this item, which had been stored away at least a decade before. The band laughed in amusement – so Crahan hung it on the front of his drum kit as a bizarre decoration.

It was a clown mask.

CHAPTER THREE

1996

Masks reveal more than they conceal. That, more or less, is the essence of the answer any member of Slipknot will give when asked why they chose to start wearing masks in early 1996. Perhaps the clearest evidence of this was visible at a session in January, after Shawn's old clown mask had been hanging on his drum kit for a couple of sessions, and he decided – on a whim, it seems – to put it on. The mask had some history, it appears. Shawn later told the Australian *Loud And Heavy* webzine how he had acquired it in the late Eighties: "I was walking through a mall in Des Moines. It was about a week or so after Halloween and there was a clearance sale of masks and Halloween gear, and that mask was sitting in there all by itself. I had $50 in my pocket – my allowance that I'd worked for – and I was with my girlfriend at the time. We were walking through the mall, and I saw that mask and it just stood out like a sore thumb and spoke to me immediately. I didn't really know what I was feeling, I mean Halloween had come and gone and I saw this thing and had to check it out. So I went over to it and put it on and I

started acting like I do with it on right now. My girlfriend started giving me some grief about how I only had so much money, and that we had to go out to dinner. We walked about the mall, and I wasn't really conscious because I was thinking about the mask and I came back and bought it and I've had it ever since."

The ensuing rehearsal was the most frenzied session yet – Crahan, always a committed performer, played and headbanged so hard that he came close to physically injuring himself. His bandmates noticed the difference: he explained that he felt able to play the part of another person while wearing the mask, and that he would continue wearing it when he played.

Slipknot had other things on their collective minds. Fresh from the confines of SR Audio, they stripped the songs back to their most basic level and attacked the rehearsal schedule with a vengeance. However, all was not well: the band arrived one evening at Anders' house to find themselves a man short. The absentee was guitarist Donnie Steele, who had neither

indicated that he would be elsewhere nor phoned Colsefni to say he was ill. After one or two more missed rehearsals by Steele, the players became concerned. In a guitar-based band – even one which dabbles in jazz, soul and other "lighter" styles – his absence was a serious handicap. The band duly took action. According to Josh Brainard: "I remember we all piled into Joe's truck to see if he was at his house - he wouldn't answer the phone – and we could see that he was there."

Mystified, the band continued as well as they could, but it wasn't until one of them met Donnie in the street that they were given an answer. Josh says, "When we finally talked to him, he said, 'I'm your friend, but I don't want to do this any more'. It turned out that Donnie felt that playing with Slipknot was against his Christian beliefs." Needless to say, the other members were a little surprised: after all, Donnie had for several years played in Body Pit, a deeply aggressive death metal band. The consensus was that Donnie must have had a religious conversion or experience which had made him uncomfortable with Slipknot. "I would have preferred that he would have told us, rather than just quitting," says Anders, while Josh adds: "I knew he went to church and stuff, so it didn't surprise me all that much – it was just *how* he did it."

Suddenly Slipknot were without a guitarist. Their biggest concern was not that Donnie had deserted or betrayed them in any way – they all accepted that a person's beliefs must dictate their actions – they were more worried about finding a competent replacement. Steele's talent was impressive – Brainard remembers him as "a pretty technical guitar player, which was something I wasn't accustomed to right at the beginning. He was one of those multi-talented guys: I remember him telling me once about these country gigs he used to do – playing banjo!"

A solution to Slipknot's dilemma soon presented itself. Joey suggested the recruitment of Craig Jones, a member of his side project, Modifidious, which had also produced Josh. Jones, a quiet man in his early twenties at the time, was an old acquaintance of the band and needed no persuasion to join Slipknot. After very few sessions, he had renewed his old Modifidious guitar partnership with Josh and the band felt that the Donnie Steele saga was safely behind them.

Soon after Craig's arrival, the band received confirmation of a second gig on April 4, this time at the Safari Club, a reggae bar. Josh laughingly describes the Safari Club as a "shithole", but qualifies this by praising it as "small and old, with a lot of good vibes". The set that Slipknot planned to play there included most of *Mate. Feed. Kill. Repeat* as well as some newly-developed material, notably a cover of 'Hybrid Moments' by the New York hardcore punk band The Misfits. "We did it slow and heavy with low vocals," he remembers. "Joey actually played guitar on it and I did percussion."

The gig went well. Craig played expertly and showed no signs of his recent entry into the band. Shawn wore the clown mask for the first time onstage: just as with the fateful rehearsal session a few months before, he behaved like a man possessed, inflicting actual damage on his drums and holding the crowd's dumbfounded attention from the beginning of the set. He also wore his welder's jacket to add some visual flavour. The rest of the band performed in normal clothing, except for Anders, who complemented Crahan's disguise by covering his face and torso with black electrical tape. This squashed his features to the point where he was almost unrecognisable, and he says, was agonising both to apply and to remove: "It hides your features a little bit, too – almost like a mask in itself." Colsefni was at his most shocking, however, during what he now refers to as his "carving period" – when he used a razor blade to cut his chest onstage, as many a driven rocker had done before him. However, he was soon talked out of this by concerned friends.

Few in the crowd expressed much surprise at Shawn and Anders' appearance. They were among the most animated players in the band in any case, and this kind of bizarre departure was almost to be expected, Crahan's clown mask – an image that has always carried horror-movie connotations: Stephen King's *It* novel is a prime example – and the obviously painful tape that Colsefni chose to wear, were a far cry from earlier masked bands such as the late-Eighties metallers Crimson Glory, who had adopted metallic semi-masks to great ridicule.

The owners of the Safari Club were so pleased with Slipknot's performance that they were offered a regular monthly slot – but some of the musicians, notably Jordison, were concerned about their image. Would audiences think it strange if only Shawn and Anders wore masks and odd

and he occasionally wore a top hat for gigs, although this didn't last long.

Craig, strangely, chose to wear women's pantyhose over his head, which gave his face a compressed, robber-like look: it was probably the most sinister mask in the band. He later switched to an even more bizarre item: a diver's helmet decorated with long steel nails, which were attached by rubber stickers to the surface of the helmet. It remains one of the most cumbersome masks – if it qualifies for mask status at all – in the band. The others soon learned to stay away from Craig onstage, and with good reason. Paul decided on the most fully-formed head-covering of all – a pig's face, made from a leathery, skin-like substance, with a large ring (sometimes complete with a padlock) pierced though the septum of its nose.

"It started for me when I came to rehearsal one night wearing a ski-mask rolled up on top of my head." JOSH BRAINARD

clothing? The consensus was yes – and so they decided on a fully-masked look. After some trial and error, each man settled on a new face.

Josh remembers, "It started for me when I came to rehearsal one night wearing a ski-mask rolled up on top of my head like a beanie hat. I just decided to pull it down over my face when we were playing." Joey Jordison had come across a Japanese Kabuki mask – an expressionless white rubber oval which gives away no clues about the wearer whatsoever. It's only his long hair, streaked with red, and his diminutive size – he is a slim 5' 4", and had therefore been the logical candidate to sit inside the Patiently Awaiting The Jigsaw Flesh sculpture – which identifies him. At the time, however, his hair was black,

Each member knew more or less what was right for him, and when the appropriate headgear wasn't available, he simply made it himself or customised an existing mask. In fact, Brainard appears to be the only one who tried out several different masks before landing on the right choice. Discarding the ski-mask immediately, he then adopted a long black robe and an executioner's hood. "It was kind of OK, I didn't think it looked very good," he says now. The hood turned out to be an annoyance when playing live, as it would slip down and obscure his vision. The band soon came up with an alternative: "Shawn said, you should try this bondage mask – and I loved it. In the shows it didn't move, it didn't get all fucked up. The other one, I would have to pull it around and fuck

with it." The mask that Crahan suggested looks nothing short of agonising: a skin-tight, black rubber affair that encloses the entire face and neck down to the collar. According to Josh: "People say, man, it must have been uncomfortable, and you know? It wasn't. For an hour I was the king of the world, man, hitting it hard. I'd open up the chin and let the sweat fall out – I really dug it."

And so it seemed, in mid-1996, that the band's new image was ready to be tested live. However, their extensive use of samples on *Mate. Feed. Kill. Repeat* proved difficult to replicate live without having a band-member who could trigger the necessary effects. An integral part of the sound, the samples

Lecter in the thriller *The Silence Of The Lambs.* Despite his fearsome appearance, he insists: "I'm not a violent person by nature. Don't fuck with me, and you'll be fine."

Craig settled into his new role as sampler with ease. One of the quieter members of the band, he has always appeared content to stand behind his equipment and control the samples via a laptop computer as the rest of the band erupt around him. Producer Ross Robinson later detected hidden depths in him, telling *Record Collector* magazine: "When I first met him he never talked. He was super-quiet and never spoke a word. I would point at him and say, dude, I bet you're the most psycho fucker in this band!

"When we're wearing all our masks, we don't have to wear a frown and look really mean. We just have to stand there." ANDERS

and other electronic effects added an important dimension to their music, and Slipknot needed to incorporate this into the upcoming gigs at the Safari Club.

The solution came from Craig, an electronics and computer buff, who suggested that he become their full-time sampler. All agreed this would be the best solution although, once again, they would be losing a guitarist. In came Mick Thompson, the hulking guitarist from Body Pit, the band in which Anders, Paul and Donnie had all played. Thompson's guitar lessons at Ye Olde Guitar Shop left him plenty of time for a band, and so in summer 1996 he became the seventh member of Slipknot. His playing, as you might expect, was expert, and his partnership with the equally gifted Josh was a guitar dream team indeed. He needed a mask, of course, and he chose a fearsome-looking brown leather hockey mask, not dissimilar to that worn by Dr. Hannibal

And he still didn't say anything. I would try to get him to talk and he would just sit and stare at me." Was he trying to freak Robinson out? "No – it's just the way he is. I started tripping on him a little bit – he didn't say *shit.* The first time he talked was during an interview with some magazine, and he said, if I wasn't in this band I'd probably be out killing people. And when he said that, all these letters of protest came in. So the only time he talked, he caused a bunch of shit!"

As Slipknot began playing regularly at the Safari Club, their new masked look began to achieve the desired effect. Josh recalls walking onstage for the first gig: "People were like, what the fuck is going on? Word spread quickly!" Within a couple of concerts, the ripple effect caused by Slipknot's new image and sound ensured that the venue was always packed for their gigs.

The new shows were radically different from Slipknot's early appearance at the

Crowbar. Now all in masks, and supplemented by the hefty, animated Thompson, they were a sight to behold: Shawn would usually wear something bizarre such as a rented nun's habit, while the others would often come onstage dressed in odd costumes such as a ball dress or a Little Bo Peep shepherdess outfit. Little wonder that audiences flocked to witness this otherwordly phenomenon. It was also a different – and perhaps enlightening – experience for the musicians: "When we're wearing all our masks," Anders said, "we don't have to wear a frown and look really mean. We just have to stand there." But all this was peripheral to the music: the relentless guitar churning and the mighty percussive attack of Jordison, Crahan and Colsefni was a sound like no other – or at least, like no other previously witnessed in the peaceful state of Iowa – and Craig's insane barrage of samples, formed of snatches of dialogue, movie soundtrack or just pure noise, added an almost tangible air of insanity to the already fairly unhinged Slipknot show. A memorable 'Craig moment' was the introduction to the concert, in which brain-addling strobe lights would come on and he would play a loop of a crazed laugh and ice-cream van bells. This would build to a stomach-shaking crescendo, punctuated by Crahan, who dropped a power saw onto the stage, creating a fountain of sparks that flew into the audience.

The shows continued, attracting the attention of the local press. The city's newspaper, the *Des Moines Register*, had on its staff at the time a journalist called Erin Kinsella, who covered the local music scene and who became the first reporter to publish a feature about Slipknot. Picking up on the buzz that had built around the band, she contacted Shawn and arranged a visit to his house. Walking into the room, she found the band seated in a circle on the floor, with burning candles, and chanting. The experience was an introduction into an unfamiliar, murky world, as she subsequently wrote:

"Individual band members have been playing for up to 15 years. They say their shared views brought them together. Until playing live a couple of weeks ago, they had been living in virtual isolation since last fall, preparing themselves, writing tunes, hammering out new instruments. Their music covers every spectrum: industrial, metal, jazz, funk, rap, disco, country. The music is vital to really express themselves, but so are the costumes, they say. The costumes reflect their personalities, not obscuring them. "If we were in an area more accepting of things, we wouldn't have turned out this way. All the bureaucracy, competition, bullshit between bands, we're sick of it," Anders says.

Interpreting Slipknot's collective decision to mask themselves is no easy matter.

If you gathered together all seven of Slipknot's masks into a pile – as was done in a memorable photo session later in the band's career – and examined them for a common theme, it's clear that many of them are associated with pain – Josh's bondage mask, Craig's skin-tight pantyhose, the constricting tape and self-mutilation of Colsefni (who would also string a painfully taut chain between his pierced, bloody nipples). Simultaneously, some are associated with horror-movie kitsch: Crahan's psychopathic clown, Mick's chilling hockey mask, the robot face of Jordison. Even Paul Gray's pierced pig-face is nothing less than the stuff of nightmares.

They've been criticised as mere gimmickry or a marketing stratagem, but the band insist the masks are a way of deflecting attention from themselves and how the media would perceive them. Fans are forced to assess Slipknot on the strengths and weaknesses of the music alone. Joey later said, "We never put on the shit we wear to try and get people into us... the music's the most important [thing]." This is a fair point, and perhaps even somewhat noble – and speaking out against the cult of celebrity is a brave move in itself in a world where the more meaningless a symbol becomes, the more the media latch on to it.

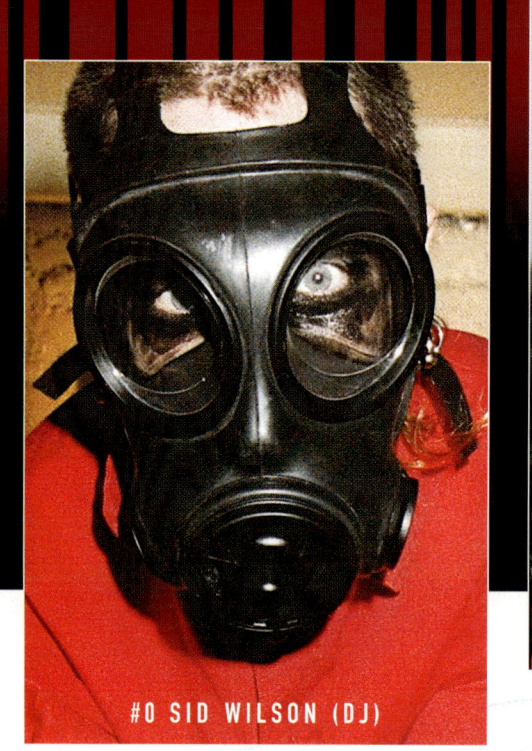

#0 SID WILSON (DJ)

#1 JOEY JORDISON (DRUMS)

"You mate to reproduce, feed to survive, kill the

#2 PAUL GRAY (BASS)

#3 CHRIS FEHN (PERCUSSION)

opposition – and then the cycle repeats itself."

#4 JAMES ROOT (GUITAR)

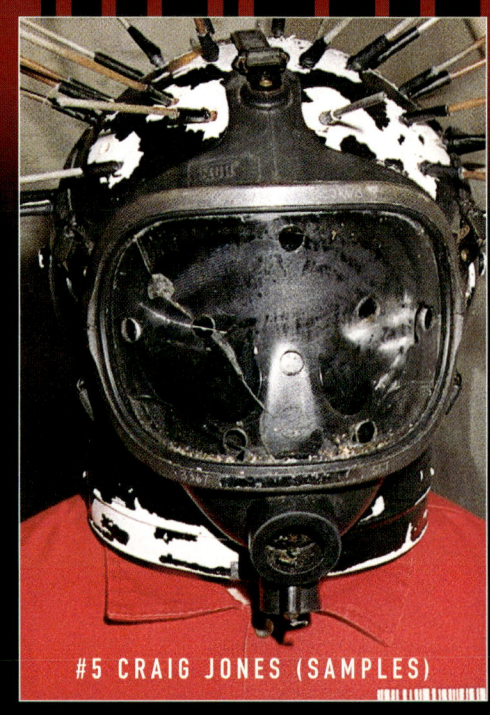

#5 CRAIG JONES (SAMPLES)

"We are not a Satan-worshipping band –

#6 SHAWN CRAHAN (PERCUSSION)

#7 MICK THOMPSON (GUITAR)

#8 COREY TAYLOR (VOCALS)

but it's not for the queasy or weak-minded."

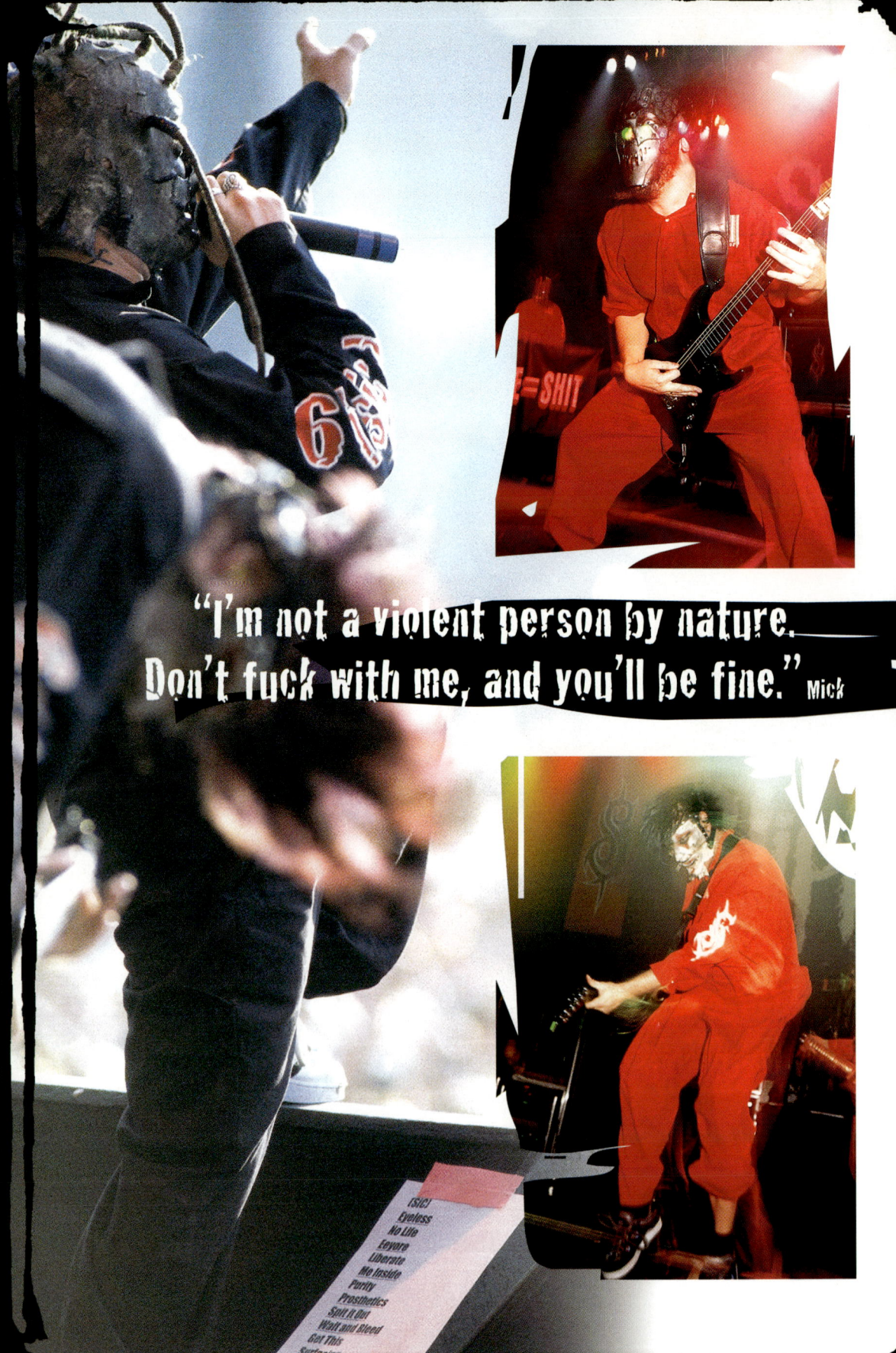

"I'm not a violent person by nature. Don't fuck with me, and you'll be fine." Mick

#1 JOEY

#0 SID

#6 SHAWN

#4 JAMES

#7 MICK

#8 COREY

unmasked

"There's no getting rid of us.
We're the virus that there's no cure for.
Because we're the virus that is the cure."

But this only scratches the surface of the Slipknot psyche. There's far more to the masks than this. For Slipknot, Des Moines had become nothing less than a modern hell, the worst of the world for a young, hard-hitting, innovative band. Culturally and politically, the city is conservative. Religion constricts behaviour and imagination. Its economy is based on rigid, traditional cycles of agriculture, and its attitude towards anything cutting-edge or unusual is steeped in caution. As Joey put it, "No-one gave a fuck, no-one cared." He later enunciated the secret of Slipknot's inner conflict even more clearly when he said, "As sick as it may sound, it goes back to where we come from... why we sing the lyrics we do, why we are so fucking pissed off all the time."

It wasn't just Joey who had things to say about the city and its attitudes, either. Anders pre-empted the accusations of devil-worshipping that he predicted would inevitably come flying from Des Moines' more conservative element, with the words: "We are not a Satan-worshipping band - but it's not for the queasy or weak-minded." The band also talked of the Slipknot experience as akin to working out accumulated poisons, the residue of years of frustration, boredom, rejection, insecurity and fear – all caused by a hostile, unchanging environment that would not and could not accept them. *This* is the horror of Slipknot – represented by the faces of the laughing clown, the S&M victim, and the mutilated, filthy animal.

There's still more, though. Producer Ross Robinson, who would later go on to work on Slipknot's breakthrough album, said in 2000 that the roots of the Slipknot malaise were not restricted to Des Moines. "There's a whole generation of kids growing up [in America] right now," he said, "who are so sick of consuming, which they are programmed to do... that they just want to fucking *destroy*. And when that anger comes out, it looks like Slipknot." Robinson went on to list the problems of the average Western youth: eating fast food, never having a meaningful conversation and brainwashed into intolerance and unthinking apathy, with the more self-aware of this lost generation feel a growing sense of revulsion at their robotic, bland lifestyle. And their solution is to worship at the altar of bands such as Slipknot, who are not better, happier or stronger than they are: Slipknot are the same as their fans, with the same sadness, the same rage and the same despair.

Perhaps Shawn summed it all up most precisely when he said that Slipknot is an army fighting a war.

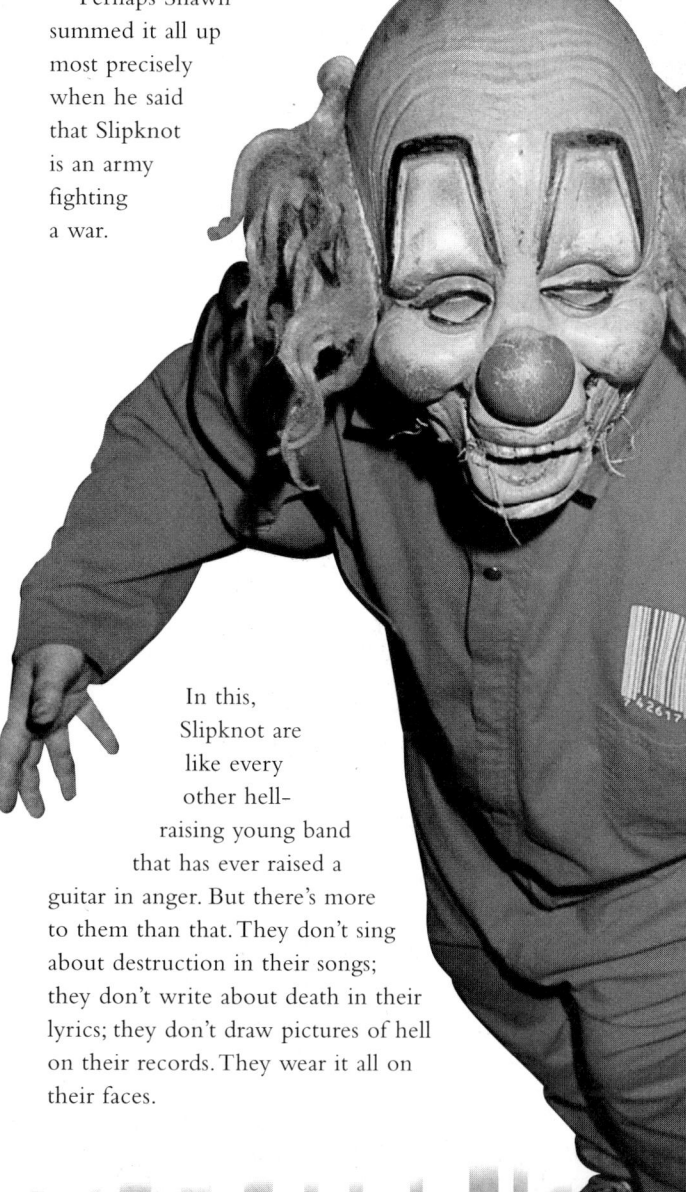

In this, Slipknot are like every other hell-raising young band that has ever raised a guitar in anger. But there's more to them than that. They don't sing about destruction in their songs; they don't write about death in their lyrics; they don't draw pictures of hell on their records. They wear it all on their faces.

IS IT METAL? IS IT JAZZ? ON SLIPKNOT'S FIRST ALBUM,
NO-ONE KNEW FOR SURE. *Reproduced by kind permission of Viz magazine.*

CHAPTER FOUR

1996 – 1997

As 1996 rolled by, Slipknot made the most of their time. The successful gigs were mounting up, a buzz was developing about them and the press were taking an active interest. They sensed they were about to make a serious impact and motivation levels were high. With this in mind, they returned to SR Audio for extended recording sessions. Although the *MFKR* tracks were long complete, the songwriting process hadn't stopped and, in fact, once the band had commenced recording, they didn't stay away from the studio for long. Mike Lawyer estimates that the band sporadically recorded and/or mixed for a period of almost three years, starting in late 1995.

So where is the product of all this work? Three years, even allowing for time off to work, rehearse and play live, is a lot of studio time. According to Lawyer, the results are likely to remain hidden for the foreseeable

future: "There's an entire second Slipknot album recorded," he says. Shawn Crahan has recently confirmed to Lawyer that the master tapes are safely under lock and key: a wise move, given that the material would be a bootlegger's wet dream. Mike does state that the songs are excellent, with some great performances by the band: perhaps Slipknot will choose to release this early material when their foothold has been established more firmly.

Meanwhile, the concerts at the reggae bar, the Safari Club, continued at the rate of one or two a month. The Safari appearances were always on a Thursday evening, and the band could not therefore rely on an audience of weekend carousers. "We used to flyer so much in this town, we were putting up three thousand to five thousand flyers," said Crahan. "The bar owner would get a call from the city saying they were going to fine him for every flyer. He'd call us, and we apologised, but he said 'Keep it up!'" This led, Crahan believes, to the establishment of a whole new music scene in Des Moines, due to the hundreds of people attracted in this way to the Slipknot shows.

The concerts themselves had developed into a jaw-dropping spectacle. The clothes the band chose to wear often contrasted with the grinding, threatening music they played. Most surreally, Mick Thompson sported a G-string and a cape, while Joey appeared in a little girl's dress and pigtails. Combined with the pig (Gray), the clown (Crahan) and the crazed, tape-smothered Colsefni, the overall image was a grimly fascinating scene. In early press reports many of the band also adopted pseudonyms: Gray was known for a long time as The Pol, Joey as Nathan, Mick as Sven and – best of all – Josh as Gnar.

A boost to Slipknot's fortunes, which was of both commercial and psychological benefit, was their participation in a "battle of the bands" competition in June, 1996. The event was sponsored by a local radio station, KKDM, and took place over three rounds at the Safari Club. Des Moines bands

such as Slipknot were fortunate to have radio shows devoted to local music: this platform remains a rarity in the UK, for example. However, the roles of radio in the two countries are rather different: the USA, with its vast expanses of sparsely-populated land, relies on radio as a promotional and communications tool far more than the more densely-packed Britain. This explains the intense rivalry that can develop between neighbouring stations in America, and which would soon feature prominently in the Slipknot story.

In this instance, KKDM hosted the competition and selected some of the city's most prominent acts, including Slipknot and their only serious rivals, Stone Sour. The two bands were scheduled to meet in the very first round. Anders Colsefni remembers, "What stood out for me was the intensity of the show, as well as the crowd. You know, Stone Sour were much more appealing to the regular people! We had strange ideas. We thought that somehow it was pre-ordained." Did he badly want to beat them? "Well, not obsessively. But Paul and Shawn and Mick were very competitive against them – they really wanted to show Stone Sour that Slipknot were better than them."

Josh has at least part of an answer. "When I was in Modifidious, they beat us in another radio Battle Of The Bands," he recalls with a certain amount of glee. So it was a revenge match, it seems. Perhaps fortuitously, *Register* journalist Kyle Munson (a big Knot fan) was among those chosen to select a winner, as was Sean McMahon. Their decision was unanimous – Slipknot were the winners.

"It was satisfying, just out of petty crap, when we beat them – I was like, well, how about that!" says Josh. Stone Sour recognised that they had been beaten fair and square and Slipknot were through to the second round. However, Stone Sour had been their most promising opponents, and after two more rounds against mostly unprepossessing bands – although Anders does remember a talented blues band called Black Caesar putting up a

valiant fight – the final victory was theirs. Slipknot were officially the best band in Des Moines in 1996.

The prize included some studio time at SR Audio (a valuable asset for the constantly-recording Slipknot) and a slot on the prestigious local festival, the annual DotFest, next scheduled to take place on June 7, 1997. All in all, the knock-on effects were far more than simply winning a teenage battle-of-the-bands contest at the village hall.

One consequence of the band's growing profile was their need for some form of manager, and the first candidate now appeared. Her name was Sophia John, who offered to take over the band's affairs for a year at no charge after the KKDM Battle Of The Bands. Despite the fact that she had never managed an act before, John turned out to be a highly competent

associate, and to this day they remember her with great affection. Anders first met her at the Crowbar: "Sean McMahon introduced me to her. She is a fiery Greek, but a very sweet one also. She throws a monkey-wrench into my distrust of all radio people." Sophia was indeed "a radio person"; specifically, the Assistant Program Director for KKDM at the time, with many contacts in the music and media business and very useful for Slipknot at this stage in their career.

Slipknot now had both Sean McMahon and John on the team, as it were, and could start to make inroads into the wider music industry. One of the first tasks was to get their recordings to the media. This meant sending out copies of the *Mate. Feed. Kill. Repeat* CD to as many useful contacts as possible – many of the 1,000 copies of the album that had been pressed were packaged up and sent out throughout the summer. Over 500 were sold at Safari Club gigs, especially after the KKDM contest had been won. This CD is extremely sought-after with copies at online auctions fetching prices of up to £150 or $400 in 2000.

Mike Lawyer remembers, "At one point, when we were sending out promo packages to record labels, we had a stack of 100 of those sitting right here – that would be worth a fortune now." This activity continued until the end of the year, when about 400 copies remained.

The response to the promo albums was fairly positive. The band's trademark blend of metal, jazz, disco and funk was a little strong for some tastes and instant stardom was clearly not on the cards for Slipknot. Nonetheless, the CDs continued to go to the DJs, promoters, journalists and record companies, and the band's determination remained at a high pitch. At a launch party

prominence certainly increased in the ensuing months and perhaps validates his claim that Slipknot "started a whole new scene".

The time had now come, it was felt, for Slipknot to spread beyond Des Moines. Their progress had been rapid and fortuitous, but the team behind the band were largely friends and acquaintances rather than professional marketing experts. Sophia John and Sean McMahon were experienced in their respective fields, but distribution and promotion of the *Mate. Feed. Kill. Repeat* album was still done on an informal basis. This changed when the Midwestern distribution company Ismist became involved.

"If we get signed, we get signed – it's not a big deal." PAUL GRAY

at the Safari Club Slipknot gave one of their most powerful performances to date, rounding off what had been a highly eventful year with a suitable bang. The venue was packed to the gills, as the band's following had been swelled by new devotees (former Stone Sour fans among them) and those who had managed to get hold of the *MFKR* album, which was even available for a time at high-street stores.

In February 1997, Shawn bought the Safari Club. The move wasn't particularly associated with Slipknot and their gigs there, although you'd be forgiven for assuming that it was. It appears that he had wanted to own a bar for some time. His renovations included the laying of a new floor – Anders Colsefni, a concrete worker, paid off his debts to Crahan for the *MFKR* recording costs in this way. The *Des Moines Register* even ran a story on Crahan's takeover, under the headline "Come on and Safari with me"

Crahan did a competent job of running the bar, though whether he made much money from it is unknown. The venue's

In May 1997 Dan, the head of Ismist, made the three-hour journey to Des Moines from his home town, Lincoln, in the neighbouring state of Nebraska to attend two weekend gigs, one with the remarkable Nashville Pussy (featuring a two-metre-tall, fire-breathing female bassist) and the other by Unsane. Both shows took place at the Safari Club. He was given a copy of *MFKR*, and asked to get in touch if he liked the music. "Slipknot were not what I would normally listen to, being based as much in metal as they are," said Dan later. "I like the punk noise thing more, but I could see working with these guys, since the two branches of music aren't that far off." After a meeting with Sophia John, Ismist agreed to distribute the remaining copies of the album – although at this point only 386 of the original 1000 copies remained.

Gigs at the Safari Club continued, and the band started to play elsewhere, notably in Omaha, where a local following began to accumulate for this bizarre, electrifying bunch of musicians. But the main focus of

activity on the live front was Slipknot's forthcoming appearance at the Dotfest, the Des Moines music festival organised by KKDM – so named because the station used to announce itself on air as "KKDM 107 dot 5".

The band spent the week beforehand practising their set to a level of precision they inexplicably called "pure tweakness", doubly valuable given that a series of regional dates had also been set up, commencing about a month after the Dotfest. At the end of the

"They're going to hate us, and we're going to force it on them."

The issue of a record deal had become an important one at this stage. Slipknot had been in existence for almost two and a half years by now: the members knew they were talented and were fully aware of the impact of their live show. With both John and McMahon working to bring industry contacts to the band, all of the people involved knew how crucial the Dotfest would be to the band's career chances.

week, Crahan seemed more relaxed about the show, commenting that, "This could be the only time in our lives we have something like this to be in. But we like to be pessimists." The always-calm Gray seemed almost blasé, responding to the point that record company A&R reps would be there with the unfazed remark, "If we get signed, we get signed – it's not a big deal." Anders also maintained an air of dark sang-froid: "I like to think the worst is going to happen," he gleefully predicted.

After all the expectation, it was no surprise at all that Slipknot's performance was among the most memorable they had ever displayed. The band slammed as hard as they could, the audience screamed like banshees and the media and label reps pricked up their ears in interest. Afterwards the band members agreed that a positive step forward had been taken.

Little did they know that the most radical shake-up yet to befall them lay just ahead.

CHAPTER FIVE

1997

Their first outdoor festival behind them, Slipknot travelled to Omaha by truck and played a handful of shows. While on tour, Ismist allocated a catalogue number to the *Mate* album – ISM CD 7-42617-0000-7 – and for administrative reasons, pinpointed an "official" release date as June 13, 1997. Responses to the recording continued to be positive and some of the songs – notably 'Do Nothing/Bitch Slap' and 'Slipknot' – received a certain amount of airplay. However, as the last of the 1,000 CDs went to the press and Ismist bowed out, having fulfilled their side of the agreement with Slipknot, it became clear that no record deal would come about on the strength of *MFKR* and the band resolved to enter the studio in the summer to record new material, ideally for a release towards the end of the year.

In an interview with the *Loudside* webzine, Crahan spelled out exactly what *MFKR* means to him nowadays: "It was a musical journey, that's all it ever was. We were in hiding for a year making music and we decided to release it. It's one thing being in a basement making music and vibing off each other, and it's another thing going home by yourself and listening to what you personally created and that's what *Mate. Feed. Kill. Repeat* was. We spent 30,000 dollars on that record. We went through a lot of different styles... It was just to see what we wanted to do."

In August 1997, an unusual discussion took place at one of the band's regular Saturday meetings. Joey and Shawn approached Anders and told him that a second singer had been recruited into the band to share lead and backing vocals. Colsefni was surprised, but even more surprised when he was told that the new singer was to be Corey Taylor of Stone Sour. According to Taylor, Shawn, Joey and Mick had visited him at the porn shop where he worked and invited him to join the band – or, as he later put it, "they basically told me if I didn't join the band they'd kick my fucking ass."

Taylor, the best vocalist of any other Des Moines band, was chosen because his mid-range singing style would perfectly

complement Anders' lower vocal parts. As Josh recalls, "The idea was to bring in Corey and have him and Andy have a kind of trade-off, Anders handling the harder vocals and Corey the melody stuff." Colsefni agreed to give it a try. Not everyone was entirely happy with this development from the first, although ultimately all came to realise that for a variety of reasons, an extra vocalist would benefit the band. Brainard remembers his initial doubts: "I was torn about it, frankly. When they first suggested it to me, I'm like, well, you know, Corey's in *Stone Sour*... but when he started singing, I was like, wow, this is really good." While he realised that Corey could help Slipknot move forward, he sympathised with Colsefni: "We talked to Andy a little about it and he was kind of hesitant at first. He was like, I'd be willing to try it, but it kind of pisses me off..."

Corey got in the band, it was like, well, he *can* do a lot of this real hard stuff. Maybe Andy can fall back and be one of the backup vocalists."

Anders confirms that most of the band knew nothing about this latest decision: "It came as a surprise to Josh. He didn't say anything and Craig didn't say anything. All Paul said was hey, look at it this way, we just pretty much broke up our biggest competition here in town. What the hell? What's that supposed to mean?" His anger was understandable, but he gritted his teeth and the rehearsals went ahead.

Brainard respects Colsefni's integrity, but points out that the recruitment of Corey was almost inevitable if Slipknot were to move onwards and upwards. "I think everyone had made their mind up that we needed to do something different, if we wanted to make this happen. We all sat down and talked about

"Corey really brought a whole new energy into everything. It's inherent in him, he just can't help it." JOSH

On Thursday, the band met for practice. To Colsefni's shock, however, the game-plan had changed again. "I found out about Corey joining Slipknot on Saturday, and then we got together and had our meeting Thursday, when Shawn tells me no, I'm *not* gonna be singing 50-50, I'm gonna be singing background vocals only, to help give some balls to Corey's voice. It was all Joe and Shawn talking. Nobody else said a word."

In fact Corey could handle both the mid-frequency singing and the guttural death metal vocals that Colsefni had made his own. Indeed, Taylor managed some impressively throaty bellows on later songs such as 'Spit It Out' but Colsefni was disappointed about his new role, to say the least. Josh: "I think once

it," he says. "Corey really brought a whole new energy into everything. It's inherent in him, he just can't help it. And he was real good at harmony, he could do all those things."

And so the revised Slipknot – now an eight-piece – approached their scheduled concerts, once again at Crahan's ever-more-successful Safari Club, in summer 1997. Time was short before the first show on August 28, and it was immediately agreed between the two singers that to save time, Corey would take the lead vocal throughout the set and Colsefni would back him up. Perhaps it was at this point that Anders should have held his ground: had he done so, the outcome might have been entirely

different. As it happened, not only did
Taylor perform most of the lead vocals, but
he also handled other conventional duties
of the frontman, introducing the songs and
whipping up the crowd. He also adopted a
mask, a leathery, bag-like approximation of a
hangman's mask; like Josh Brainard's bondage
mask in that it covers the entire head and
collar, but much less defined. To solve the
problem of fitting his long dreadlocks into
the mask, he cut holes in it and threaded
them through. Much later – after a year or
so – he found that this did his hair and scalp
no good at all, and cut them off, reattaching
them to the surface of the mask for a much
easier ride. He also uses face make-up:
a black (or sometimes red) substance that all
the bandmembers apply to the exposed areas
of their faces under the masks – some areas
of skin around the eyes and mouth remain
visible. However, this can often mely
on-stage: it's not designed to remain solid in
high temperatures, such as underneath a
tight-fitting mask.

It was clear that Corey had attained a
particular personal goal by joining Slipknot,
the envy of the Des Moines metal scene.
He became known immediately for his
commitment to the band and its aims, stating
as his express wish the desire to "infect
everyone that needs to be infected." He also
commented that the way forward for his
new band was "First, kill everybody, then
total world domination will ensue." Oddly
enough, he introduced himself in early
interviews as Faith. No-one seems to know
why, though presumably it's along the same
lines as the band's insistence in those early
days on writing their name SlipKnoT, rather
than the simpler Slipknot – an initial fad
that lost its importance as time passed and
the band found its feet.

Other press reports were just as
enthusiastic. "By appearances you'd think
Corey died and came back as a different
man... he showed at least six very distinctive
vocal styles," remarked one journalist.
The media weren't just concentrating on

Taylor, though: Anders Colsefni was as
much under the spotlight as ever, claiming,
"It was crazy. It was weird. I'm not singing as
much, but I am moving more and beating
on the drums more. I thought I was going
to be a lot less tired than I normally am, but
I was wrong."

Nevertheless, all was not well, and
after two shows as a backing vocalist, Anders
decided to quit the band. He recalls the
build-up to the decision. "I felt completely
backstabbed and betrayed. It was really bitter
for me. Part of the reason why I ended up
quitting was because I wasn't getting to sing
hardly anything – Corey was singing all
my words, and he didn't have any idea what
he was singing.

"It bugged the hell out of me, so I just
quit. At the end of the show one night, at the
end of the last song – 'Scissors' – I made an
announcement. I said this was the last time I
was gonna be playing with Slipknot. I didn't
tell anybody in advance. Shawn just looked
over and jumped down and sat on the floor."

Did you discuss it afterwards?

"No, they pretty much acted like they
knew I was gonna end up quitting. Shawn
didn't talk to me for months and months.
He left after that and he wouldn't talk to
me at all."

Was this ever resolved?

"No. Not really."

How serious was Anders about leaving
the band he had worked so hard to establish?

"When I made the conscious decision
to quit, I wanted to do it on my own terms.
I wanted people to remember the night
I quit, so I did it onstage. I went out with
a bang, because I don't think we'd ever
played 'Scissors' with as much energy before.
To prepare for my last Slipknot show,
I shaved off my eyebrows and most of my
facial hair. The eyebrows took three months
to grow back. I was serious."

Josh Brainard remembers this fateful night
well. "To tell you the truth, I was a little
pissed off right when he first said it. I was
just mad, because he punked us out on stage:

I felt it was unprofessional. I think Shawn was real pissed off for the same reason." It didn't take Brainard long to come to understand his motives: "When I thought about it a little bit, I thought it was maybe what *I* would have done in his position."

Does Josh think that Shawn later realised that Anders perhaps had the right to feel that way?

"Yeah, sure. We really wanted him to stay in the band, we wanted him to do the drums and the backup vocals, that would have been really cool." This statement puts to rest any sneaking suspicions that Anders or anyone else may have that Corey was introduced to the band with the intention of replacing Colsefni. Josh goes on: "But I can't really picture that scenario any more, because what Anders is doing now is so fitting for him. This is what he was *meant* to do."

He's talking about Painface, the band which Anders almost immediately went on to form with several other Des Moines musicians. They're an uncompromising, versatile outfit which benefits from the full range of the Colsefni voicebox and at the time of writing has released a successful self-financed album, *Fleshcraft*. The definitive Anders touch is, of course, the lyrics, many of which continue to refer to the old *Rage* characters – not so much a hobby for him, or even an obsession: it's nothing less than a way of life. Colsefni remains on good terms with Slipknot. Shawn and Anders meet whenever the former is back in Des Moines, and Colsefni also contributed guest vocals to Corey Taylor's 2001 solo album, *Superego*.

After Anders' departure, Slipknot regrouped and considered their position. A release of some kind had been been on the cards since the previous year: the band decided to return to SR Audio and record new material, as well as redoing the vocals of some of the old songs. Like the 1996 sessions, these recordings remain something of a mystery: the producer Sean McMahon has stated that these tracks – except for one, 'Spit It Out' – will remain hidden in perpetuity. "The only track that's ever been heard is 'Spit It Out'. Shawn has recently mentioned that he might try to convince the record company to let him remix them and maybe put them out. Because it has some great performances on it: they have the feel that 'Spit It Out' has on it," says Mike Lawyer.

Corey's recruitment came at a tricky time for the band. According to Josh: "We were actually preparing to release the updated version of *MFKR* when Corey joined the band – and that really turned things on their heads." Not only did the band elect to re-record the entire set of vocals for the album – an expensive, time-consuming process, not made any easier by Corey's unfamiliarity with the Slipknot dynamic – but Taylor is a powerful force for change in his own right, which meant that Slipknot needed to adjust to him as much as he had to adapt to them.

The first mention of 'Spit It Out' in the story is timely. An accusing, bile-ridden track, it was written – according to popular legend – in response to the growing rivalry between the two principal Central Iowan radio stations, KKDM 107.5 (where manager Sophia John was now Programme Director) and KAZR 103.3. Corey, growing tired of this, wrote the song as a retort.

Slipknot were now Des Moines' leading band and, because they were allied to Sophia John, their music received a lot of airplay on KKDM (or "the dot", as it was known). KAZR allegedly resented this and named their own 'hot band', a genuinely talented act called 35" Mudder, with which Slipknot has never had issues. This attempt to pit the two bands against one another was transparent and, it seems, pretty shallow. Also, both stations were competing for the same audience share, which meant that occasional insults would be traded and that loyalties from anyone associated with either station were necessarily more binding.

All this juvenile nonsense would never have affected Slipknot's rise to prominence

had it not been for two important events. The first was KAZR's response to KKDM's successful and much-anticipated Dotfests, of which there were three in 1997, '98 and '99: a similarly-scaled outdoor festival called Mancow's Lazer Luau. The title referred to the host, a well-known KAZR disc jockey called Eric "Mancow" Muller, whose talk show was an entertaining fixture of the KAZR schedule. Out of loyalty to Sophia John and KKDM, Slipknot didn't play at the first Lazer Luau. The record deal they were ultimately to sign coincided more or less with the decline of KKDM as an alternative radio station: it's thought that the definition of alternative music had become so blurred

decision and alleged that Slipknot had circled one of his colleagues and threatened him. Sophia John responded rapidly, stating that in her opinion Mancow was not responsible for this, but also that she had suffered the indignity of having the words "fat fucking cunt" written on her car by enemies in the business. It's not surprising therefore that Slipknot felt the need to write 'Spit It Out'...

Life for Slipknot moved on. Rehearsals and gigs continued (notably, the band would perform an all-ages show at the Safari Club on January 31, 1998, as a thank-you performance for the Des Moines fans who had been neglected since Slipknot had been

Cuddles made a point of destroying as much of the set as possible during the shows, and would even dismantle his drum kit and throw it into the crowd.

that the market couldn't sustain two stations, and ultimately KKDM became – and remains – a mainstream broadcaster. After this, KAZR became a Slipknot supporter, championing their cause as a local band made good, and so the Knot inevitably performed at the second Lazer Luau on July 31, 1999. But that's jumping ahead to a completely different era – in Slipknot terms, anyway.

The second, more serious incident occurred when Slipknot had been scheduled to play at a concert at the United Center in the big city, Chicago. It was to be hosted by Mancow on Halloween, 1997, and featured Anthrax as headliners. However, a last-minute decision was made to pull Slipknot from the bill – a galling development for the band, who knew that the gig was a chance for serious exposure. A director at KAZR, Mancow's station, blamed Mancow for the

playing in Omaha), the band completed their new and modified recordings, and airplay and press coverage mounted. However, since Colsefni's departure, the all-out percussive assault of the Slipknot drummers had necessarily weakened somewhat. Initially the plan had been for Corey to do as Anders had done, and combine lead vocals with the extra tribal percussion. In practice sessions, he had proved that he could play the drums with as much ferocity as anyone else and at first, it seemed that this would be the way forward.

Josh had other ideas. "I said, guys, we really need to get another drummer." The idea that Taylor would be a frontman free to run around the stage, as he had so effectively done in Stone Sour, was attractive – but only to Brainard, it seemed. "They were like, no, screw that! We can do it!" He sniggers as he remembers. "And then we

practised a couple of times like that and they were like, you know what? You were right!"

The man eventually chosen to fill Anders' shoes was Greg Welts, a long-time friend of the band who worked as a tattooist at Dave "Davo" Wilkins' shop, The Axiom. Welts had previously been in a punk band with Paul Gray called The Havenots, and his work adorned the bodies of many of Slipknot's friends and acquaintances – Colsefni in particular had felt the Welts needle on

almost insane character, he made a point of destroying as much of the set as possible during the shows, and would even dismantle his drum kit and throw it into the crowd. Occasionally his maddened personality led to him being called Giggles by the rest of the band.

The end of 1997 saw Slipknot make their second appearance on an album. SR Audio's Mike Lawyer had organised a 24-track CD of central Iowan bands for

more than one occasion. Greg had tattooed four large panels onto Anders' back, the beginnings of a comic strip showing the change of a man into a wolf – those *Rage* themes once again. More significantly, it was Greg who inked the Slipknot logo, a bendy S, on Colsefni's leg. Anders says now that it was just a quirky dollar sign until it became the Slipknot symbol. The band had also included a photo of Welts on the inside tray of the *MFKR* CD case, thanking him in the credits list along with Wilkins.

Greg – who chose to wear a baby's mask on stage, and was duly given the nickname Cuddles – joined the band in September. His presence was immediately felt: a driven,

charity. All the bands were recorded live by Lawyer at the Safari Club, on the nights of November 8 and 9. 'Spit It Out', which had been circulated to the media and which was receiving widespread local radio airplay, was included, as was 'She's An Actress' by Joey's sporadically active Rejects. The album was released as *State Of Independents Volume 1*, cost a mere ten dollars and generated funds for the AIDS Project of Central Iowa. Sponsors included the usual suspects KKDM, the studio and the venue, as well as *Muzi.com*, a webzine that flourishes to this day.

It was the last Slipknot recording not to sell in droves.

CHAPTER SIX

1997–1998

"It's up to the clown to intimidate me and keep me in line." SID WILSON

As Slipknot edged towards their third year of chaos, heads started to turn in far-off places at the spreading reputation of this band from the middle of nowhere. The biggest coup in the Knot's career to date occurred when Sophia John persuaded Ross Robinson, the producer behind Korn's self-titled debut and Sepultura's recently-released *Roots* album, to work with them.

Asked today how he first came to hear of Slipknot, Robinson is incredulous. "Sophia called my manager out of the blue," he told *Record Collector* in 2000. "My manager was the first one she tried. She said, I'm trying to find who looks after Ross Robinson. And he said, you know what? I manage him!" After messages had passed between Robinson, his manager and Sophia, Ross agreed to drive down to Des Moines and meet the band, who would rehearse for him.

Robinson was not only a skilled producer but also an A&R man and talent scout for the New York label Roadrunner which had always been at the forefront of heavy metal, specialising in speed metal in the Eighties (Sepultura, Malevolent Creation, Carnivore) and death metal in the early Nineties (Deicide, Obituary, Brujeria). From the mid-Nineties, however, the label has moved more towards nu-metal, industrial and other crossover acts which incorporate punk and electronica into their sound, such as Coal Chamber, Fear Factory, Glassjaw, Machine Head and Life Of Agony. It was at the top of the metal-label tree – and in 1997, Ross had signed a unique deal with them. Roadrunner allowed him to produce three new acts per year through his own imprint, I Am Records, with no pressure from the label with regard to budget or recording style. Roadrunner would fund, manufacture and release the

albums; in return, the bands signed in this way would be officially contracted to Roadrunner, with I Am the intermediary.

In March 1998, Robinson arrived at Shawn Crahan's house. The weather was very wintry, with banks of snow everywhere, but to Robinson's surprise, the members of Slipknot were sitting outside waiting for him, despite the freezing weather. "When they saw me coming," he recalled gleefully, "they jumped up and ran inside. Like a bunch of little kids! It was really funny..." They were keen to display their most brutal, technical side to Robinson, and he immediately understood the Slipknot message. Josh Brainard says, "He really dug it. I could see his wheels turning." Robinson had also heard parts of *Mate. Feed. Kill. Repeat* but wasn't

event showcasing unsigned and newly-signed artists, a chance for record company executives to take in the nation's hot new acts in Nevada's City Of Sin. The band snatched at the opportunity – Las Vegas is, after all, several universes away in cultural terms from Des Moines – and the gig was set up.

Before this could happen, however, one final addition to the line-up needed to be made – a DJ. Decksman Sid Wilson, of a loose DJ collective called the Des Moines Sound Proof Coalition, had struck Slipknot as appropriately loopy. It was a relief, as Josh points out: "We'd actually talked about it for a long time, but we didn't know anybody who could do it – the people we knew who were DJs all sucked!"

"If that's the future of music, then I want to be dead." UNKNOWN A+R MAN

impressed. "I heard it, and I thought no, I don't think so," he says today. His perception of Slipknot was based almost entirely on one rehearsal – and what a powerful session it must have been. And slightly crazed, too: as he entered the rehearsal space, the band shouted "Girl in the practice room!" – a meaningless statement which they always yelled when a non-member was present.

To the band's delight, Ross offered to add them to the I Am roster and produce an album in the near future. Brainard recalls the sense of relief that flooded through the band: "Ross was a big card in the industry, and when the labels heard that he was going to produce a record for us, they were like, sure – we'll work with them."

Ross also arranged for Slipknot to play at a Las Vegas festival on May 15. The show, a multi-stage event called Gameworks EAT'M (pronounced "Eat 'em" – actually Emerging Artists and Talent in Music), was an annual

Ross Robinson laughingly describes Sid as "a rave kid, not from the hip-hop scene. Before he joined the band, he took 75 hits of acid in one day or something – he still sees trails sometimes." Wilson became the second maddest member of the band after Crahan – rapidly earning the sobriquet Monkey Boy – and has in fact developed an apparently genuine on-stage rivalry with the Clown. The two men will lock eyes across the stage, spontaneously leave their equipment and attack each other with real violence – a violence based, from what they both say in interviews, on mutual affection. Wilson said in 1999, "It's up to the clown to intimidate me and keep me in line."

Sid joined the band's live frenzy with worrying commitment, lending weight – as we shall soon see – to Robinson's added comment that "He jumps off really tall objects, too." His choice of mask was a military gas mask, heavy and constricting,

that he uses because it prevents the onset of what he refers to as Organic Syndrome, a genuine or fictional malady that he claims causes him to hate people whenever oxygen enters his skull. This is perhaps one of Slipknot's least plausible claims – but it's insane enough to satisfy the fans as to the reasons behind his apparent madness.

The addition of a DJ to the line-up isn't as odd as you might think. One of the concepts behind nu-metal is versatility, or a kind of plurality of musical influences. Sid's recruitment to Slipknot was a reflection of this growing trend, just as much as it tied in with the band's own agenda, which revolves around the motto of "If it sounds good – play it."

In May, Slipknot travelled to Vegas for the

Roadrunner's Senior Vice-President of A&R, Monte Conner. But Conner wasn't as easily won over as his colleague: "He kept coming out and saying, they're not ready yet," says Lawyer.

It wasn't easy, as Shawn later told *Loudsides*: "At that time we were having a lot of hard times with labels, because Roadrunner was interested, and we had bigger labels that were also interested, but then they would come to the show and get scared. The famous quote [from an A&R man] was "If that's the future of music, then I want to be dead" and we would say "We *are* the future – and we're going to fucking kill you.' "

Another label to make advances was the mighty Epic, who came very close to

"We are the future – and we're going to fucking kill you." SHAWN

EAT'M festival, a memorable occasion with over 150 bands – chosen from over 700 contenders – playing on 15 stages on the Las Vegas Strip. The local impact was significant, evidenced by the fact that Vegas' premier radio station, Extreme 107.5, added 'Spit It Out' to its *Cagematch* playlist. This show places songs back-to-back and invites listeners to phone in to vote for their favourite. Unsurprisingly, the Slipknot song won every challenge for five weeks, after which period the station retired it undefeated.

Back in Des Moines, A&R representatives from various record labels had started sniffing around, alerted by Ross Robinson's involvement that something was happening in this least prepossessing of cities. Robinson's client, Roadrunner, knew what was happening and, still uncertain whether they wanted to sign the latest I Am act, sent A+R man John Kuliak who reported positively to

offering Slipknot a deal but withdrew at the last minute after one of their execs had unresolved doubts about the band's ability. The small but influential Noise label, based in Germany but with an international network of offices, expressed an interest too. Rotten Records, the label set up by the old-school punk-metal crossover act DRI, was also in the running at one point – Slipknot had once supported DRI and a relationship had briefly existed. Even Sony made contact with the band, but negotiations went no further as they only wanted to release an EP, not a full album or string of albums. The *Des Moines Register* also reported that Interscope, Geffen, Columbia and Maverick had also expressed interest in the band.

All this activity spawned plenty of speculation in the local press, with the names of Roadrunner and Ross Robinson flying around. At one point Sophia John was forced to issue a statement, confirming that "It is

true that [Slipknot] are negotiating with two major labels, but Roadrunner is not one of them." She hoped progress would have been made before the Dotfest 2 festival (scheduled to take place on June 12) when an announcement could be made. "They have good writing, solid shows, publicity in newspapers, and even now some airplay. What they're doing is so unique... Our first goal was to make one million copies of its new album; now it's three million. I want the whole thing for them; I want the dream. I want to see them on the cover of *Rolling Stone*, playing at the Ozzfest and [setting up] its own record label. Then they can come back and grab the local bands that supported them."

With all this positivity in the air, Slipknot decided to make their image more universal by wearing red jumpsuits for a more cohesive, team-like image. Matching garments were ordered – with black and blue versions to follow (not orange: Shawn thought this would be too prison-like) and the band began to consider how to decorate them. Much later on, green, grey and white suits were added to the wardrobe – although perhaps the white option was an unwise choice, bearing in mind the mud, stage dirt, blood and other unsavoury liquids which are

splashed about by the Slipknot players in a typical set.

This apparently simple cosmetic decision led to far more profound changes. With a uniform that blended the musicians into a unified whole, they felt they were able to make a fairly profound statement to the music industry – and the fans – about the nature of celebrity and the various approaches to the fame that success inevitably breeds. They knew that record companies, no matter how innovative their culture, would treat Slipknot as a product to be marketed and developed. The band opted to pre-empt this and *become* that product before the process could be taken out of their hands. This involved discarding the members'

as well as making a statement about the inevitability of "productionisation".

It would be naive, however, to infer from this that by adopting what appeared to be an anti-commercial position, Slipknot have avoided all progress towards individual celebrity – or even that they intended to do so in the first place. They must have known that ultimately their names would be recognised and that in the end – although this has yet to take place, a remarkable achievement considering the intense publicity which continues to surround them – their faces would also become known. Even if both names and faces could have remained secret, the band must have had the foresight to know that their very 'non-celebrity' would

"We busted our asses for two years!" COREY

individual identities, a process initiated by the adoption of masks back in 1996. Each man chose a number: the band agreed collectively that in interviews they would refer to each other only in this way. Sid Wilson, the new DJ, became #0; Joey Jordison, #1; Paul Gray, #2: Cuddles, #3; Josh Brainard, #4; Craig Jones, #5; Shawn Crahan, #6; Mick Thompson, #7; and Corey Taylor, #8. The band have since said that each player chose the number that meant something special to him, with no conflict whatsoever.

The next step was to identify themselves as a product. This was done in the simplest way possible: the bar code that Ismist had allocated to the *Mate. Feed. Kill. Repeat* album – 7-42617-0000-7 – was stencilled on the right sleeve and back of every jumpsuit. The band are said to have purchased the legal rights to the number, although how this was done remains unclear – surely it's difficult to copyright a sequence of numbers? Whatever the method, the band took in this way what was initially an effective stance against the cult of celebrity which they sought to avoid,

be marketed and used as an image. As it has been, in fact: the masks and the jumpsuits *are* Slipknot's recognised trademarks. But the concepts behind the image seem to be based on a genuine desire not to pursue the well-trodden path to fame – and for that, they deserve a measure of respect, irrespective of their music. What's also gratifying is the fact that the band don't usually refuse to pose for unmasked photos with fans who request a picture. They normally obscure part of their faces with their hands or any object to hand such as a CD, or they put on a hat and bow their heads forward: but one of their stated aims has always been to remain accessible to their audience, so they tend not to refuse photos on principle. Corey said once that photos are taken of them without masks almost every day, with or without their consent. His only caveat to the photographer is a request that the picture be kept private. Mostly this has remained the case, although it's possible nevertheless to track down several unmasked photos on the internet.

The second Dotfest at the nearby town of

Ankeny – and the first outing for Slipknot's new look – occurred as planned on June 12. The new look went down well. The crowd welcomed the addition of Sid, who slammed as hard as any of the other members between dropping in some inspired breaks. It was one of the last concerts that Slipknot would ever open. Big-time success beckoned, but not before yet more internal turmoil.

Sometime in late June or early July, word arrived that a formal offer of a $500,000 recording contract would be made to Slipknot by Roadrunner, who had finally decided to sign them. The band's response was ecstatic, as you might imagine: the reward for all their labours – as Corey later put it, "We busted our asses for two years!" – had come home at last. It was arranged for a formal contract signing to take place on July 8. To commemorate the occasion, the players decided to put pen to paper in the open air, at a venue special to them: outside the Axiom tattoo and piercing parlour. The press were informed and a sense of anticipation started to build. Slipknot's associates, of course, were delighted. Sophia John in particular felt as if all her efforts had finally borne fruit. She had noticed the band's change from a backroom outfit to a fully professional crew, too, telling the local press, "What I saw then, what I see now, is different. [Slipknot] have elements of pop and can be marketed on the mass appeal level."

On July 6, just days before the signing was due to take place, Cuddles was asked to leave the band. It's not clear why he was fired, and no-one is prepared to discuss the issue. The silence can be attributed to the fact that legal processes are still in motion. Anders says that because Cuddles was fired from the band, he sued them in response, but more than that he wisely chooses not to reveal. Josh confirms that Cuddles was indeed fired, but is similarly reticent, as the following conversation illustrates:

Do you know why Greg was kicked out?
"Yes."
Can you say why?

"I don't know" (laughing).
Because it might be libellous?
"Yes."

Neither will be drawn – which is fine: it's a sign of their professionalism. Greg Welts himself has proven impossible to track down, although one internet rumour suggests that he is now running a tattoo shop called The Ultimate Prick in South Dakota. And there, unexpectedly, the story of Cuddles must end...

Nonetheless, Slipknot's signing to Roadrunner took place as planned amid much rejoicing. "It was a seven-album deal," explains Josh, "one of which could be live and one of which could be a greatest-hits package." Five hundred grand sounds like a lot of money, of course, but as Josh points out, that doesn't go into Slipknot's pockets: "You don't *get* that money. That's $500,000 against the recording and distribution of seven albums. People have a hard time digesting that!" In other words, Roadrunner would fund the making of the records and a percentage of the subsequent sales revenue would find its way back to Slipknot. The players themselves would – like almost all modern bands – make most of their money from touring, merchandise sales and publishing revenue from commercial use of their work. How newly-signed acts survive until money starts coming in is not normally the record company's concern, although in most cases an advance is made to the band against future royalties.

The *Register* reported: *One important clause in this contract stated that the band retained 100 percent of its song publishing rights. If anybody uses a Slipknot song (for a TV commercial, for instance), the band members will receive all the profits.*

But typical of recording contracts, most of the leverage falls on the record label's side. A sample line in the contract reads: "The masculine gender used herein includes the feminine and neuter genders." In other words, Crahan can't quit the band, undergo a sex change operation and release a solo album as a female version of his Clown character.

It could happen – this *is* Slipknot we're talking about here. In the meantime, however, the musicians continued with their everyday lives. Shawn was still running the Safari Club, Josh was a Unix systems administrator for a major IT firm, Paul worked for Shawn, Joey lived at home with his family – having stopped work to concentrate on the band – Mick gave guitar lessons at Ye Olde Guitar Shop and the others worked in various jobs. This air of almost unbroken normality – the band had not, after all, embarked on a hedonistic spending spree on signing, as so many others have done – is perhaps due to the fact that Roadrunner and Slipknot are so well suited.

The initial studio date of August 31 had been suggested, but was put back by some months in order to allow the band to hone the songs they would take to Ross Robinson's studio in California.

Now, it seemed, the band's entry into the spotlight was only a matter of months away.

CHAPTER SEVEN

1998–1999

Once again, Slipknot found themselves without a percussionist. Replacing Cuddles would not be easy: along with Shawn – and lately, Sid - he had been one of the most visually striking performers in the band, just as Anders Colsefni had been before him. Luckily, the band's ever-increasing network of musical contacts – built up after years of playing in an incestuous scene comprising several bands – yielded a candidate: Chris Fehn, who played drums in a band called Shed. Coincidentally, Chris had once auditioned for Colsefni's band Painface. A friend of Mick Thompson's, Fehn was a player gripped with aggression on stage and can be seen nowadays not just banging his head but slamming his entire upper torso up and down – in effect, headbanging from the waist up.

He happily agreed to join the band and arrived at rehearsal with a bizarre head-covering made of an all-over fetish mask – like Josh's bondage mask, but with a white, riveted face – with a long, Pinocchio-like nose attached to it. This is made of rubber and swings from side to side when he shakes his head: he also uses it to make gestures that suggest masturbation. A proud addition to the Slipknot ranks, then...

Ross Robinson giggles when he recalls Chris's initiation into the band. "They were so hard-core on that poor guy. It's still going on, too." Chris's first gig marked him out as a crazy man, though: one of his mad onstage leaps saw him destroy the venue's coffee machine. That's not too bad, you might think – just a coffee machine? Yes, but this was a professional espresso machine and cost ten thousand dollars. History does not record the club owner's reaction.

Compensation claims aside, Slipknot's task was to prepare for the awesome task of recording a 'proper' album, a record which would make the painstakingly-assembled *Mate. Feed. Kill. Repeat* seem like a mere demo. With this in mind, the band hit the rehearsal room with renewed vigour, finishing off the arrangements for the new songs, completing lyrics and deciding on the running order for the as yet untitled album. It would be a 15-song record, with one or more hidden tracks, it was decided.

Luckily, to some extent the band were aware of Robinson's recording style, which was an organic method focusing more on the spirit and the atmosphere of the songs rather than a technical stand-point. This would suit Slipknot's multilayered approach very well.

The studio they were to use was Indigo Ranch, situated in the hills of Malibu in California, a vintage affair with plenty of weathered, analogue equipment. For a band like Slipknot, which focuses on the vibe of a record or a concert and despises the commercial veneer of so many bands and the industry itself, the choice of both producer and studio was perfect.

As a side project, Craig set up a Slipknot website, which he would later manage when

germ of an idea occurred to him...

On September 29, 1998, Slipknot left Des Moines for California. They had a remarkable amount of equipment – there were nine band-members now, remember – but luckily the newly-recruited Chris Fehn owned a powerful truck into which all the gear was squeezed. "It took four days to get there," recalls Josh with a snigger. "We had to drive pretty slow. I really don't think Chris's truck should've been pulling all that weight."

The Malibu studio itself is a remarkable place. Josh continues, "That place, Indigo Ranch, is really surreal. To start with, it's on top of a mountain. It takes you forty minutes of your life to get anywhere."

"All the gear is vintage," Robinson told

"You can't see California without Marlon Brando's eyes!" UNIDENTIFIED VAGRANT

he had time. A couple of months later Shawn organised a second site, on which he planned to focus on more left-field, animated content – this is yet to materialise, but when it does come fully online it will no doubt be a twisted, visceral experience.

In between rehearsing for the new album in Des Moines, Slipknot visited Roadrunner's New York offices to meet the record company staff and fine-tune some of the strategies that the label would use when working with the band. The trip was uneventful, apart from a chance encounter on a Big Apple street with a homeless person, who was obviously suffering from a kind of dementia: as the band walked past him, they heard him shrieking some kind of strange, repeated warning. Listening more carefully, they made out the words. He was screaming, "You can't see California without Marlon Brando's eyes!" Mystified, the band kept walking – but the words remained in Corey's mind. Once back in Des Moines, the

Australian journalist Adrian Pertout, "and there are just *endless* amounts of extremely great stuff. You know, there's like over six hundred guitar pedals alone, and an assortment of microphones that is better than any studio in the whole LA area, maybe the world."

Brainard relished the physical beauty of the location, but it's clear that he and perhaps the rest of the band became restless during the six weeks that Slipknot were there. "The front yard has a view right down onto the ocean – it's amazing. But apart from the music, most of our excitement was going down to the grocery store and getting food! It was hard being there and not being able to go anywhere – well, you could, but it was a pain in the ass." The accommodation doesn't sound too unbearable, though: "We stayed in what's called a chateau, which is a place detached from the studio. A couple of us slept out there and some of us in the studio." Actually *in* the studio? "Right in it. There's beds and couches and stuff."

The sessions usually started in the early afternoon and went through to 10 p.m. or midnight. As many bands discover – and especially acts that have several players, each with a part to record and re-record – most of the time spent in a studio is wasted time, or time when you can't leave because you might be needed, but if you stay you may not be needed after all. This leads to boredom and frustration, no matter how attractive the location. Some people – like Josh – can work this off in various positive ways. "They had a grand piano in there that Paul Simon or someone had written some famous song on, so I used to go down and play that at night."

Evidence of the high pitch of excitement which the band had reached, even before

long if Chris hadn't had such an adverse reaction to it," says Josh. "I think that's why they stuck it in and said, keep watching this, Chris, this is great!" The percussionist's response was extreme, but believe it or not, the overall impression is one of a party or a relaxed gathering of friends. Just another little incident in the life of the Knot – but this time recorded for posterity.

The following day, sessions began in earnest. It didn't take long for Slipknot to become familiar with Robinson's production techniques. He's not a technical obsessive, nor a man who will sacrifice feel for precision: his choice of the resolutely analogue Indigo Ranch studio as his preferred working location reveals much about his affinity for

"He's like a complete fucking dork metal-head just like we are." JOEY JORDISON

recording could commence, can be found just before the hidden track on the album. The song, 'Eeyore', is preceded by a few minutes of recorded conversation, shouts and laughter. On first hearing this cacophony of sound, it's not clear what's happening: but as you listen, you can pick out one member in particular, who is shouting in horror at something he can see. Others are laughing at him and giggling in what seems like disgusted amusement. Shortly, someone starts to retch loudly, while the others continue to laugh hysterically. Ross told *Record Collector* what was happening in an interview in late 2000.

"They're making Chris watch a shit video," he affirms with a chuckle. Is it specifically a shit-*eating* video? ("Dude, pretend it's pudding!" says one of the people on the track, in between gales of helpless, nauseated laughter.) "Yes!" replies Robinson. "They wanted to be hard-core on him."

"I don't think it would have gone on that

warmth and ambience in his work. As he told Pertout, "The main ingredient is definitely capturing the soul of the artist, the spirit side, not necessarily the tones or perfect pitch and all that, it's definitely peer spirit on tape... I think that the listener communicates more with the heart and accepts it more, because it's personal."

"I have fond memories of Indigo Ranch," says Josh. "Working with Ross was really great. I really liked his production style – he really pushes you and gets you psyched up." That's something of an understatement – Robinson later said, "When the red light goes on, I try to make them forget that it's on, I grab them and punch them. Really hard. I want to take them to that place inside them – it's primal." He famously threw a potted plant at Joey's head in the middle of a take: the drummer ducked as the plant exploded on the wall next to him, but soil still went in his mouth. "Someone put it in the corner, hoping I would throw it,"

continues Ross, "but I threw other things as well!" Despite all this apparent aggression, Robinson is a calm, centred character with a genuine sense of humour – a person rather like the musicians of Slipknot, which may explain why to this day they refer to him as the band's tenth member.

In a later interview with MetalIndex.com, Joey said of Robinson: "The good thing about him is that he's our friend so there is no extra pressure on us. He's like a complete fucking dork metal-head just like we are. It's just so easy to work with him and he got the best performances out of us that we never imagined possible. He didn't really change any of it, like he does with other bands, and didn't manufacture fake sounds. He's just cool."

Shawn is also quick to heap praise on Robinson, calling him "an amazing producer", but he also recalls the hunger of Slipknot to make their record. In the first day, he claimed, seven drum tracks were completed – an unheard-of occurrence for a band as percussive as Slipknot. Robinson, Crahan said, literally had to force the band to stop recording, or the album would have been completed too soon, without the players having the chance to play themselves into the right mentality. Joey later told *Terrorizer* magazine that "he had me playing so hard, I had seventeen blisters on one hand and

nineteen on the other – my hands were wrapped up like the fuckin' mummy. And this was just in pre-production!"

In the end the recordings took until early to mid-November, although in January to February 1999 the band spent more time at the studios redoing certain parts and mixing the album. As for the record's title, it was apparent from the first sessions that there could be no other option than to christen it *Slipknot*.

After the recordings had finished and the band had bid a temporary farewell to Robinson and Indigo Ranch, Slipknot returned to Des Moines, aware that a profound experience had enveloped them. Six weeks is a long time to spend in a studio, especially at the fever pitch levels of motivation that had possessed the musicians. The players returned to their various jobs – Josh to his office, from which he had taken a leave of absence in order to record the album, Mick to his guitar lessons, Joey to his home and the others elsewhere.

Only Shawn had no place to go except home:

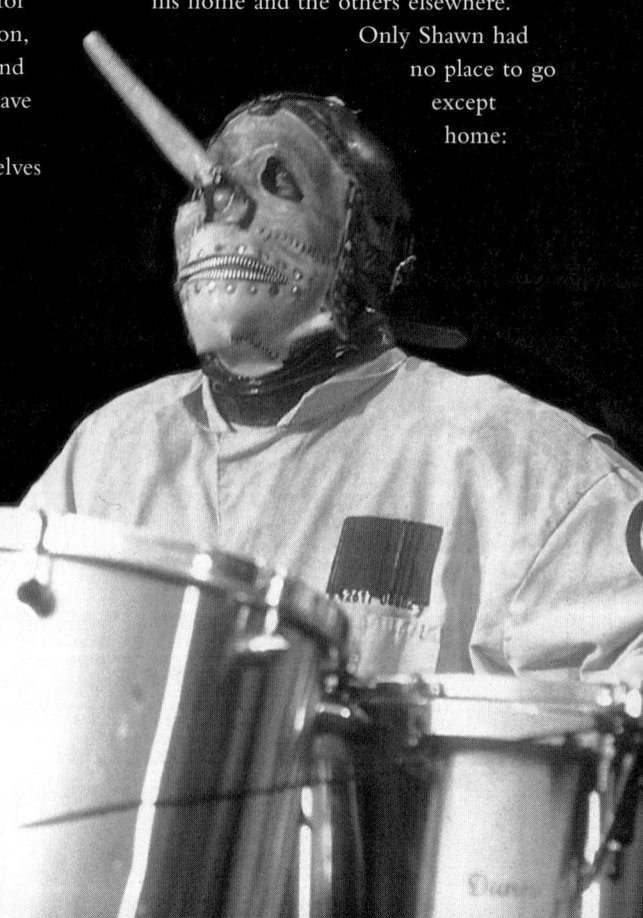

he had sold the Safari Club and was able to spend some time with his wife and young children before the studio – and a full year on the road – would call again. It was a period of rest, but not one that would last.

Just as before, the stability of the band was about to be put in jeopardy. For reasons that are still unclear to anyone outside the band, Josh decided to leave. This was unexpected indeed, most of all by the other members of Slipknot. Ross Robinson has said that the others begged him to stay – and who can blame them? After such a long time in the band – longer than any of the current line-up except Shawn, Paul and Joey – Brainard was one of the foundations of Slipknot. His playing and songwriting was exemplary, and losing him would be an upheaval more serious than any except the Colsefni/Taylor episode.

Today, Josh chooses his words carefully when asked why he left Slipknot: "I don't know how much of it I really want to comment on. But after we got done with the record, we took about a month off and started practising again..."

He pauses to think before continuing. "I guess some decisions were made that I wasn't particularly happy with. There was a lot of stuff that all came out and I said, you know what? You can have it." He laughs ruefully. It's clear that the decision was painful, but also that whatever the reason, leaving the band was the right thing for him to do at that time.

The perceived wisdom is that he left the band because he didn't want to tour and leave his family behind while he went on the road. Dozens of websites state this very clearly. "I can tell you that that has *nothing* to do with it," he says. "I think... I don't know whether the band started it or not. I'd like to think they didn't, but it did *not* come from me. I think what it

RIGHT: JOSH BRAINARD'S REPLACEMENT: JAMES ROOT

came from was, someone needed an answer when there wasn't one, and it was like, *(adopts dopey voice)* well, he probably didn't want to go on tour because of his family. That had nothing to do with it."

He draws a deep breath. "There were just some things that happened that I wasn't particularly thrilled about. I can't really be specific. I would love to be, but I can't be."

It's clear that he bears the band no ill-will whatsoever, so whatever happened up there in the mountains can't have been down to a personal falling-out. As he points out, "You know what? Those guys are all my

Do you ever have moments when you think, it would have been nice to stay in the band?

"No, not really. Everything happens for a reason."

You sound as if you have no regrets.

"Oh, absolutely. If nothing else, I've made connections in the industry."

He has indeed. Josh's new band, Undone, is building a following in Des Moines and the area — just as his old band was doing five years before — and is receiving critical praise for its technical, funky music.

Reeling from the loss of Josh, but

"Our opinions and agenda for the band grows together as people leave and come in. A common goal starts to form, you follow the same star, same pot of gold." COREY

friends, and I don't have anything bad to say. I guess where I leave it with other people is, it's between me and them. Everybody that's in the band knows why [I left], and that's kind of where I'd like to leave it. I don't want to tarnish their image or anything like that — that's the last thing I wanna do. I absolutely respect all those guys."

Are you still friends with them?

"Absolutely. I still visit with them when they're in town. A couple of weeks ago they gave me my platinum record that we all got from the *Slipknot* album."

Did he receive his share of the royalties?

"I told them I didn't want any money."

None at all?

"None. When I left I asked if I could keep my amp. That was all I wanted."

Presumably that was quite a hefty slice of money you turned down there?

"Yeah. But for me it wasn't about the money."

determined to finish what they had started so auspiciously, the members of Slipknot regrouped and returned to Indigo Ranch in January, 1999, to complete the recording and mixing. It was going to be an earth-shaking milestone of an record, they realised, after a few weeks away from it: Robinson had done a tremendous job of bringing the beast out of them and capturing it on old-fashioned tape. Proud and somewhat shell-shocked, they made their way back to Des Moines to learn that Sophia John had managed to secure them a slot on the most eagerly-anticipated freakshow of the year — the Ozzfest. This would begin in August, and although Slipknot wouldn't be playing on the whole of the tour, they were moved and honoured to be playing alongside the festival's host of renowned metal acts.

Before they could cast their minds so far forward, however, there was the pressing issue

of finding a replacement for Josh. Once again, by consulting their address-book of friends and acquaintances in the Des Moines area, his successor was located: James Root, sometime guitarist for Atomic Opera and more lately of a band called Deadfront, was the man selected. An excellent player – and, like Mick, a huge man at 6' 6" – Root was delighted to be offered a place in Slipknot and found his niche within a matter of days.

I played one show in it and it really sucked. I was like, 'No, fuck this mask. I'm going to do something new.'" This he did, getting hold of a white, demonic jester's mask which is one of the most visually striking aspects of the formidable Slipknot parade.

With this final personnel change the line-up stabilised and remains unchanged at the time of writing. James has now been in the band for two years and no other member

The mask he was asked to use, however, was less pleasing: Josh's old bondage hood, still sleek and murderous-looking despite the years of abuse, was extremely difficult for him to wear. Although Brainard had found it comfortable and even inspiring, Root found it impossible to breathe easily or even wear on stage with any degree of comfort. Monitoring his friends' progress from the sidelines, Josh later commented that he didn't find this surprising: "I think the mask is a part of me, and that's a big reason why it didn't work for Jim. That just wasn't his personality. That's why the mask always made him sick. It was similar to a body rejecting an organ transplant."

James told the *IGN For Men* website: "The bondage hood was really painful.

of Slipknot looks like leaving. It's a close-knit unit, more along the lines of a family than a band (Corey told the *Register*: "Our opinions and agenda for the band grow together as people leave and come in. A common goal starts to form, you follow the same star, same pot of gold. We've all got the same type of sense of humor, coolness, what kind of music we like. I've joined a family, not a band,") the members will defend each other in any interview, never revealing any inner conflict or strife. Maybe this is one of the reasons for their subsequent success: the fact that from the outside, they are a team. Perhaps a twisted, strange team, but a team nonetheless.

On Monday, June 29, 1999, the *Slipknot* album was released worldwide. In Des Moines, the band sat back and waited.

CHAPTER EIGHT

1999

It is the failing of youth not to be able to restrain its own violence.

(SENECA, 3 BC – 65 AD)

Make no mistake: *Slipknot* is a brutal album.

It begins with an eerie, sampled background drone, overlaid with what sounds like a looped, distant scream. After three seconds a gabbled, high-pitched voice starts repeating, "The whole thing, I think it's sick." This is the first track, named '74617000027' after the *Mate. Feed. Kill. Repeat* bar code which the band have stencilled on the arms of their jumpsuits. The stomach-fluttering ambience in the background comes straight from the equipment of Craig Wilson, while Joey confirmed in an interview not long after the album's release that the voice – often rumoured to be a snatch of film dialogue – is in fact Corey's, speeded up until he sounds like a young or middle-aged woman. A mere 36 seconds in length, the track builds and builds – with the ominous drone swelling

and waning all the time – until the sound drops away suddenly, allowing the voice to mutter its crazed, meaningless mantra one last time.

There is a split-second pause.

The sound which then erupts from the speakers is the essence of Slipknot, the core of modern metal, and the very sound of distilled rage itself. It is the opening riff of '(Sic)', a reworked and much accelerated version of the old song 'Slipknot', which opened the *MFKR* album – and most of the band's live shows – and from which the band took its name. The eight bars of this enormous riff are the hammer with which the band batters its audiences into immediate submission. After two bars of guitar and super-tight percussion, Jordison makes his presence known further with a barrage of double bass drums playing sixteenths – the evidence, if any were needed, that his tastes

JAMES ROOT

and experiences tend towards death and black metal. Taylor enters the song with a roar of pure aggression on the cusp of a riff change, before addressing a screamed manifesto to an unidentified "enemy", warning "don't you fuckin' pity me!" and winding up to the final repeated horror that is "you can't kill me, 'cos I'm already inside you..." The original lyrics, which began "Pentex sucks! Pentex sucks!", were growled by Anders Colsefni over a much slower, more deliberate version of the song. Robinson and Slipknot obviously chose to speed the whole thing up (although through repeated live performances, songs tend to speed up anyway due to the onstage adrenaline), brighten up the sound – particularly the snare drum and guitars – and replace Colsefni's original fantasy-oriented sentiments with more threatening, aggressive lyrics. It's Joey's favourite Knot track, which says something about its enormous power.

The third track is 'Eyeless', based on an insane chorus lifted straight from the words of the deranged vagrant encountered by Slipknot on their trip to New York. In an unprecedented move for a metal band, Slipknot elected to start the song with some understated scratching from Wilson and a treated, possibly electronic percussive accompaniment: this is a snare and kick-drum pattern more akin to drum'n'bass than any more metallic style, kept low in the mix and not echoed on the rest of the album. A wailing, two-string lead riff is then heard and the rest of the band come in until a full, driving sound is achieved, leading up to the frantic, gabbled chorus: "You can't see California without Marlon Brando's eyes!" The highlight of the song is a slower, more considered riff based on a precise string-bend by guitarists Brainard and Thompson and bassist Gray, which Jordison confessed later

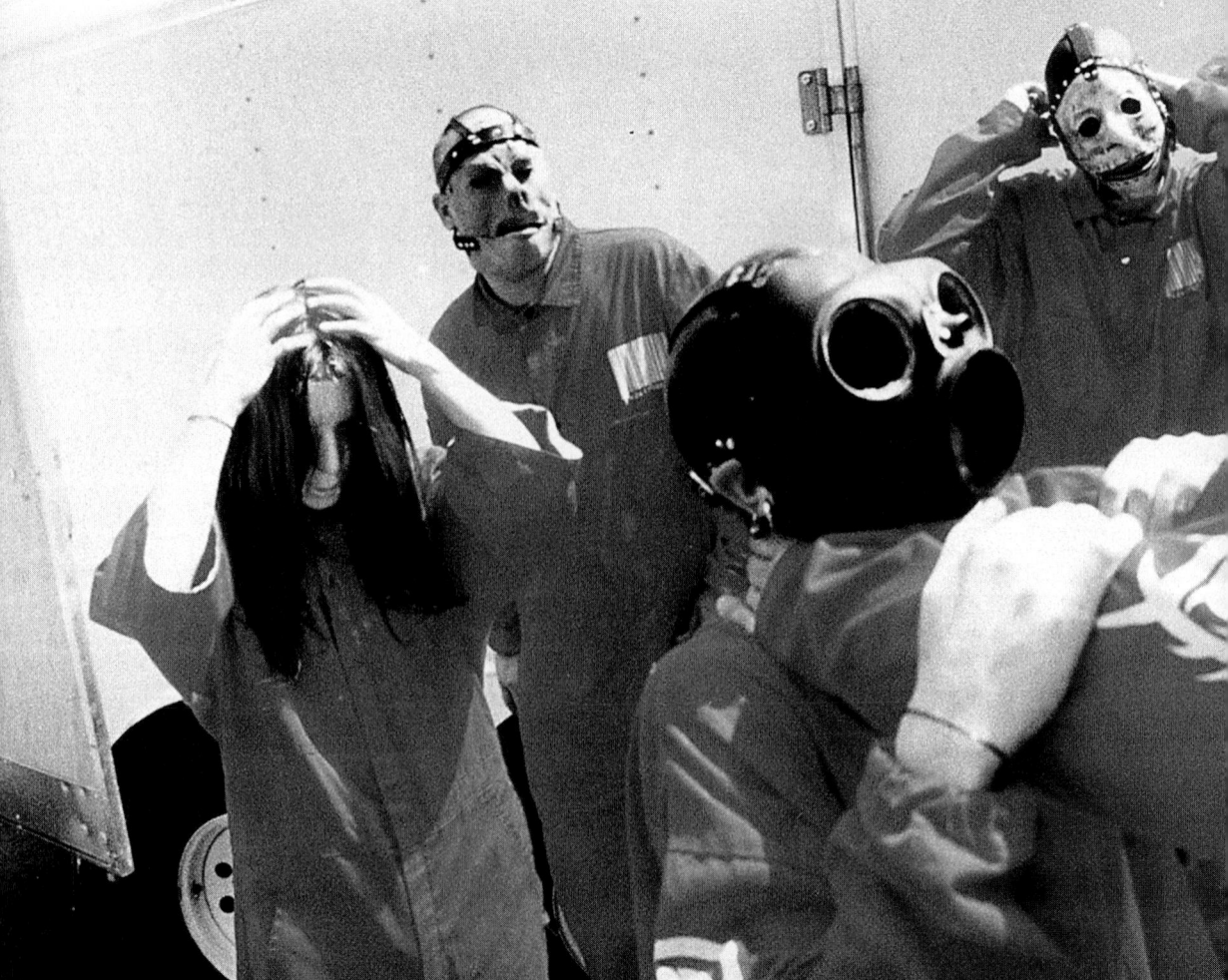

on was heavily influenced by Morbid Angel. This appears halfway though the song and then again at the end, in a much sicker, dragged-out form, approaching the numbing, deathly-slow tempo of grindcore and the perfect accompaniment to Taylor's throat-shredding plea to "look me in my brand new eye". Lyrically, 'Eyeless' showcases Corey at his most confessional: the line "I am my father's son/'Cos he's a phantom, a mystery and that leaves me *nothing*!" is a clear explanation of one of the singer's more obvious preoccupations.

'Eyeless' is one of the most arresting songs on the album, and fans and press have continually pressed the members of Slipknot for a definition of its meaning. Joey – normally the one elected to try to answer this question – has never been very exact on the matter, telling the BandIndex.com interviewer: "It's not necessarily about Marlon Brando's eyes, it's a pivotal figure of Marlon Brando being the untouched guy that he is and 'eye' being such a strong word, because that song is about Corey's dad and how he doesn't know him. So we're using a figure that everyone knows, to amplify the song and with California being such a big fucking state. Like we just use them as articles or examples of a picture. Like the whole motto is, unless you're going to be strong enough or realize what the outcome has been in life, don't try to see something that you're not going to fucking see." Clear? Me neither.

There's a change of pace, it seems, on the live favourite, 'Wait And Bleed': its intro is gentle and even sensitive, with Corey singing a clean, melodic vocal over a simple guitar and bass sequence and a calmly hissing cymbal from Joey. When the song proper begins, Jordison adopts a rolling, tom-tom rhythm, and like many great songs, even though the intro, first verse and chorus are the same four lines, the melody is truly memorable. Corey is singing from the perspective of someone who has cut their wrists in a suicide attempt and is waiting for death. Heavy? In all senses, although the song is among the most hummable of the Slipknot canon.

a rebellious self-identification by Corey; or simply a general warning to back off.

'Spit It Out' is the only track to make it to the public's ears to date from the 1997 sessions with Sean McMahon which Shawn Crahan has safely under lock and key. McMahon is credited as the producer in the *Slipknot* sleevenotes, and there is a perceptible difference in its overall sound in comparison to the later, Robinson-produced material. The closest to rap-metal that the band have approached in their post-Colsefni incarnation, the song begins with a hollow, treated riff and a gabbled, caffeine-driven line from Taylor: "Since you never gave a damn in the first place / Maybe it's time you had the

Slipknot welcome the dispossessed, the wronged and the resentful as part of their army of fans.

According to the band, 'Surfacing' has had a profound effect on many Slipknot fans, who recognise its vicious chorus of "Fuck it all / Fuck this world / Fuck everything that you stand for" as a statement made to anyone who is hostile, uncaring or simply on the wrong side. Corey even introduces it live as 'the new national anthem'. Slipknot welcome the dispossessed, the wronged and the resentful as part of their army of fans (or 'maggots' as Joey calls them. Why? Because they feed off Slipknot) and understand their anger and frustration. As Ross Robinson had said, there's a whole generation out there who just want to destroy... It's a powerful song, whatever the message, with an insistent lead line running through it and a disturbing, rumbling bass part: Joey's drums are also extremely upfront. "I am the push that makes you move" may sound like a fitness video slogan, but in this context it's an odd, somewhat unsettling repeated threat. It can be read as a promise that Slipknot will change the listener's life for the better;

tables turned / 'Cos in the interest of all involved I got the problem solved / And the verdict is guilty!" The same riff continues through the song, going through louder, smoother and rougher versions: what's most interesting about the song is that Corey alternates between a very low Colsefni-style baritone on the lines "Spit... it out" and the melodic counterpoint, "All you wanna do is drag me down / All I wanna do is stamp you out!"

The next track, an updated recording of 'Tattered And Torn' from *MFKR*, is superior in many ways to the original and one of the most atmospheric songs on the album, making full use of Wilson's insane sampling and Corey at his most deranged. Vocals are multi-layered – there are at least three tracks on the song – to create a hellish environment of weeping, wailing and bellowing voices.

The next two songs were inspired by the story of Purity Knight, an American teenager who is said to have suffered an appalling death at the hands of an unidentified

murderer sometime in the late Nineties. The story, run by a popular US entertainment website – and still online at the time of writing, for those who are diligent enough to seek it out – posited that Purity had been abducted and buried alive. Before her death she was able to leave a handwritten note, which was later discovered by the authorities. Horrified by the story, Slipknot wrote two songs, 'Frail Limb Nursery' and 'Purity', which followed 'Tattered And Torn' on early copies of the album. However, shortly after the record's release, Slipknot were informed that the entire story was fictional and

minute, and is a grim, depressing experience.

'Purity', which started life as 'Despise' (a demo version of which was included as a bonus track on the digipack version of the album) is much more structured. Opening with a powerful, industrial riff and Gray's stomach-shaking bass, the song is punctured with dreamy, ominous semi-spoken lyrics from Corey, which build to an echoing, almost anthemic chorus of "You all stare, but you'll never see / There is something inside me". Lines such as "I am in a buried kennel / I have never felt so final" would seem to indicate that the song is indeed based on

"Prosthetics" is a clanking, sinister song which appears to be sung from the perspective of a murderer or stalker – perhaps there's a pattern emerging about the band's areas of fascination?

therefore the intellectual property of the website that had created it. The band and Roadrunner responded to this by reissuing the album in December 1999 with the two tracks replaced by another song, 'Me Inside', which had originally appeared as a bonus track on the limited-edition digipack edition of *Slipknot*. The two erased songs can still be tracked down in MP3 format on the internet for those who didn't pick up the early version of the album. To this day, however, no-one seems to be sure if the Purity Knight story was genuine or invented.

'Frail Limb Nursery' is, like the opener, '74617000027', a collage of jumbled sounds rather than a song in the conventional sense. This background ambience, a group of echoing, electronic samples accompanied at the end by some faint percussion, lies behind a tearful spoken-word narrative by a teenage girl who would appear to be a friend of Purity's. The whole thing lasts less than a

Purity's story, but the rest of the lyrics are oblique enough for some uncertainty to remain.

'Me Inside', which replaced them, was more accessible: opening with some hushed ambience, the band break into a military-style riff (with some amazing double bass drums from Jordison) and some of Taylor's most aggressive lyrics to date. As the album progresses, the singer's anger becomes tinged with a kind of sadness or self-pity. The line "Fall on my face, but can't you see? / This fucking life is killing me!" could be interpreted as a cry for help – or it could simply represent Slipknot messing with your head. The chorus, however, is the band at their most melodic and commercial, with Corey demonstrating a range not heard on other tracks. The song ends with a demented vinyl squeal from Sid, whose presence throughout the album is generally more subtle, and the Spanish line "Somos feos,

69

apestamos y pero reinamos, joto motherfucker!" – which translates as "We're ugly, we stink, but we reign, faggot" plus the usual "very metal" expletive, giving Spanish teachers across the USA a new way of motivating their students...

The same passionate venom can be heard on 'Liberate', a stop-start guitar-and-sample driven song. 'Liberate my madness!' screams Taylor, who at times appears to be free-associating with his lyrics: whoever the target of lines such as "Hard eyes glow right in my darkness again / With the sickness, renegade sisters, blisters / Salivate, litigate, liberate, madness, sadness" may be, it's clear that he's not out to make them feel good about the situation. The song alternates between the aforementioned hard-driving riff and a slower, one-note grind, with a more atmospheric feel.

'Prosthetics' is an older song: Anders Colsefni was originally involved in a much earlier version recorded at SR Audio. Although the precise nature of the samples has changed on the updated version, it is still a clanking, sinister song which appears to be sung from the perspective of a murderer or stalker – perhaps there's a pattern emerging here about the band's areas of fascination? – in which Taylor emotes with jaw-dropping involvement. In fact, Joey later revealed that the song lyrics were based on the narrative of the Sixties film, *The Collector*, based on the novel by the British author John Fowles, in which an obsessive sociopath kidnaps a beautiful teenage girl and keeps her in his house until she dies of pneumonia. The repeated mantra of "Damn it man, I knew it was a mistake" and threatening lines such as "You won't bother me if you let me bother you" make this one of the most ominous songs on the album.

There's a brief respite of sorts on 'No Life', which is nihilistic rather than downright misanthropic. The pace is stepped up (the previous two songs were among the slowest of Slipknot's material) and the song is reminiscent of Nine Inch Nails or even Gary

Numan's later, darker work. However, despite the electronic presence and the chaotic feel of the percussion, it's a metal song through and through and the main guitar riff - a rumbling, fluid creation probably courtesy of Gray, who "writes the fuckin' baddest riffs" according to Robinson - is held down with iron discipline. Corey, of course, is on violent, questioning form, warning "Save this! My rage is bliss! / I'm takin' names and gettin' pissed!". His main theme is to protest against the life he or his narrator leads - "This is no kind of life" - and the effect is unrelentingly paranoid.

The darkness continues on 'Diluted', which is formed around three discrete high points: a riff containing another death metal-like false bend, a crunching, trebly bass line and a weird sample sounding exactly like a shot from a blaster in *Star Wars*, or (just as likely given the age and cultural obsessions of the band) a lower-budget trash-culture icon such as the *Battlestar Galactica* series. The song is in a way the extension of the self-questioning morbidity of 'No Life', with its helpless question of "What the hell did I do to deserve all of this?" and a raging final shriek from Taylor of "Fuck!"

The middle section of the album is composed largely of unceasing riffing, so it's a pleasant surprise when the opening sounds of 'Only One' are a skewed electronic melody that you might expect to find on a film soundtrack. A re-recorded track from *Mate*, the song retains the best parts of the original version: the opening bellow of "Pain – made to order!", an unexpected, virtuoso tempo change and perhaps the album's most frightening moment, an absolutely murderous repeated roar of "Only one of us walks away!" The message? Corey is annoyed – don't make him annoyed with *you*.

The final listed track is 'Scissors', the song with which Slipknot always used to end their sets and before which Colsefni announced his departure. A bass-heavy song with riffs punctuated by reverberating percussion from one or more of the three drummers, the song

also contains a classic Slipknot horror-movie
moment: the muttered, threatening repetition
of "Biding my time until the time is right"
until the singer realises that "It's time" and
works up to a cacophonous peak of rage.

And then, of course, there is silence,
broken after eight minutes by the soundtrack
to the grisly initiation of poor Chris Fehn.
Then there's the hidden track, 'Eeyore',
noticeably different from the rest of the songs
on the album. Slipknot's love of punk is
well-known, and on this song the guitarists
abandon the strict confines of metal riffing
for some unrestrained power playing.
The second verse features some snare-drum
blastbeats by Joey – in which the snare
plays sixteenths along with the bass
drum, a remarkably taxing style
– and Corey's lyrics (which
he explained once as a
reference to a persistent
moshpit troublemaker
– a "Thor type" with
long blonde hair,
who enjoyed
punching those
around him, both
male and female)

are pure aggression, but without the
ruthless self-analysis of the earlier songs.
In comparison to the heart-wrenching
seriousness of 'Eyeless' and 'Scissors', 'Eeyore'
sounds like a group of thugs having fun
with casual intimidation. Needless to say,
Taylor's invective is not without a certain
semi-offensive eloquence ("Oh the fucking
sacred heart of Jesus / Blew it in the back
room"), and all in all, it's an eye-opening way
to end the record.

The album's final moments are a mass of seething riffs and broken-down electronic snarls, punctured by a "Take that, motherfucker!" sample and vanishing abruptly into the ether when Robinson delivers the *coup de grace* by pulling the plug. The listener is left frozen in shock.

This was the album which was presented to the world's music critics in mid-June 1999, and shortly afterwards, to the fans. Rage and confrontation are the primary themes. From Corey's focus on his 'enemy' in "(Sic)" and his warning to "Stay the fuck away from me!" in 'Eyeless', via the "When get my hands on you / Ain't a fuckin' thing you can do" line in 'Surfacing' and "You can hide if you want / But I'll find you" in 'Spit It Out', to the teeth-clenched "Only one of us walks away!" in 'Only One', the album is full of aggression.

the general collapse of the natural buoyancy and optimism that young people used to feel was their birthright. Call it the lack of a feelgood factor, call it a fall in standards. Call it what you want – but the decay that Slipknot write about is the decay that surrounds us, in every part of Western society.

Robinson narrows this down further: "Des Moines is all that. People are so depressed because they're just bombarded with consumerism, it's all consuming and consuming. People don't talk when they eat. They eat fast food. When people sit down and talk over a meal, it's like, what's going on? When you finally find an outlet for all this, it looks like fucking Slipknot. Or Amen. It's finally *giving* something, after taking and consuming all your life and being programmed to consume. These bands are pretty much a ministry for these people,

Rage and confrontation are the primary themes.

The third consistent theme of the album is a general preoccupation with corruption, waste and sickness. Listen to the robotic repetition of "The whole thing, I think it's sick" in the opening track – this can be read as an immediate manifesto. The band are right – many listeners thought the album, the band and their performances *were* sick, as we shall discover. Key words are shit, sick and fuck – all of which appear dozens of times across the album: it's organic, visceral and very human stuff. But none of it is gratuitous. Each scream, each curse and each droplet of verbal poison which Slipknot directs at its listeners is there for a reason: the band's profound rage and horror which they feel at the world which surrounds them.

Perhaps Ross Robinson encapsulated it best when he said: "There are a lot of kids that have no regard, they're microwaved consciousness. They hate everything." This, then, is the malaise behind Slipknot's work –

so they can release that kind of energy without hurting anyone."

The last piece of evidence of Slipknot's need to invoke the image of human waste (and humans *as* waste) is the slogan which they started to use soon after the release of the album: People = Shit. This somewhat misanthropic statement soon caught the imagination of a generation of nihilistic metal fans, who plastered it all over their clothes and their bedrooms, to the despair of a nation of parents. Asked to explain it, Joey referred it back to good old Des Moines: "I guess it just comes into the over-compulsive personalities everyone has. When someone tries to test us we will go above and beyond to make sure you leave with some sort of distaste in your mouth. As sick as it may sound, it goes back to where we come from, why People = Shit, why we sing the lyrics we do, why we are so fucking pissed off all the time."

Shawn had a more specific definition of the People = Shit concept. Speaking to a German interviewer for the *Sweet Suffering* publication, he argued: "You know, people *are* shit! Is it the Earth's fault there is pollution? No! That's man's fault. Is it the building's fault there are bombs in it? No, that's man's fault. Anything that is wrong in this world, you can blame man for it! All the oil poured in the ocean... who *made* the fucking oil? Who dug it out? People have the possibility to change everything, but most of you guys take it easy. Men have the answers to change the whole world, but until people change

social, political, cultural and anthropological significance of it all, one question remains. Is the album any good?

Fortunately, the answer is yes. Resoundingly so. It's a well-constructed, solidly-produced recording, which testifies to the talent of the performers, the songwriting skills of the composers and the instinctive feel of the arrangers. Channelling the concentrated rage of nine people – and a pretty pissed-off producer – into a set of songs, without making them unbearable, is no mean feat. For example, there are three percussionists on the album, but three drum

everything, people equal fucking shit!"

Gloomy stuff, perhaps – but not all negative or hopeless. There's positivity in Slipknot and their music: a determination to rise above it all, to make good the inner sickness and become better than their enemies. It takes dedication to see this. Perhaps this is why the band refer to their fans as 'maggots': naming followers after a repulsive creature might be construed as an odd tactic by many, but in fact the fans lap it up, posting messages such "Call yourself a true maggot?" on newsgroups, bulletin boards and so on.

But after you've pulled the lyrics and their deeper meanings apart and analysed, discussed, considered and reflected on the

tracks on every song would have been tedious and over-emphatic: however, both band and producer had the sense and restraint to hold back and play when strictly necessary. There's no showing-off or pointless noodling on the album: it's tight, disciplined and streamlined – which gives it its power. Lyrically, the band were neither naïve nor over-intellectual: the imagery they use is gripping, communicating the band's message more effectively than any direct polemic.

It's an elemental, ground-breaking record. Any fan of cutting-edge music from the turn of the millennium *must* have it.

Little wonder, then, that it went gold before the summer was out.

CHAPTER NINE

1999–2000

Immediate critical responses to the Slipknot album were positive: examples of the reviewers' blown-away reaction included comments such as "You thought Limp Bizkit was hard? They're the Osmonds. These guys are something else entirely. And it's pretty impressive," from Rick Anderson at the *All Music Guide*, and "The band's second LP is metal with a capital M, brutally intense and totally fucking scary," from Jenny Eliscu at *Rolling Stone* magazine. Commercially, the response was overwhelming: thanks to the impressive distribution power of Roadrunner, the album landed in thousands of record shops worldwide in a short period of time, and sold over 20,000 copies in the first week in the USA alone. Chart positions were also encouraging: the album went into the normally metal-phobic UK chart at No. 20, an achievement that no-one at Roadrunner had expected. The post-album saga of Slipknot had begun – and it shows no sign of abating.

In fact, the sequence of jaw-dropping events that has led to the band's current reputation as the most insane live act in the world had commenced well before the album was released. It was arranged for them to play on the Ozzfest that summer, before the album was even released. On hearing the news, the band and label began to consider how their name could effectively be brought to the public's attention without a record in circulation. The decision was made to use a company called Streetwise Marketing to distribute free cassettes of 'Spit It Out' and 'Surfacing'. 50,000 were manufactured and handed out at concerts by major metal acts before the Ozzfest started to roll. The use of 'street teams' (a concept involving marketing at grass-roots level, introduced by underground labels and adopted by Roadrunner with gusto) ensured that the Slipknot name would not be entirely new to the audiences who would come to see the festival. This was a clever move. When a new band has some devotees already in an audience, and can see its name on fans' T-shirts and hear them shouting its name and the lyrics of its songs, the psychological burden of having to win over a crowd is much easier to bear.

FRONT-ROW AUDIENCE MEMBERS LOVE SHAWN CRAHAN

The bands which would accompany Slipknot – who were, understandably, placed low on the bill – included Fear Factory, Deftones, Primus, Rob Zombie, Slayer, Godsmack and System Of A Down: a veritable galaxy of metal stars. As Slipknot embarked on the festival's first dates, they marvelled at how they had climbed so high in what seemed like such a short space of time.

Almost immediately, they made their mark, with the aggression we have seen on so many occasions causing headlines in the music press. On June 8, the first of many self-inflicted injuries occurred at the New Jersey stop of the tour, when Shawn Crahan, flinging himself around the stage and headbanging like a man possessed, accidentally butted his custom-made titanium drum kit. He required five stitches, which he received after the show at the nearby Bayshore Hospital. However, in true madman style, he finished the set first, which took place in front of a raging crowd at the unromantically-named PNC Bank Center, and even signed autographs for fans before climbing into the ambulance. Appropriately enough, the unfortunate headbutt took place during 'Eyeless' – as he so nearly was.

The fun didn't stop there. A couple of shows later he did it again, this time at Seattle's Gorge venue. On this occasion he needed 17 stitches to close the wound, which extended from the end of his nose to his forehead. He was also mildly concussed – it had clearly been a much more serious blow than the first. Thankfully, before Crahan could make it a hat-trick and fracture his skull, Slipknot's place on the tour came to an end and the band travelled home, with some war-stories already under their collective belts. In fact, Crahan's injuries have gone on to include a bruised pelvis (from his partially successful back-flip attempts), broken knuckles (from punching his drum kit), a dislocated shoulder blade (from attacking the percussion) and a damaged finger (from an early encounter with the angle grinder he occasionally deploys on stage). No wonder he needs a rest from time to time.

Shawn needed 17 stitches to close the wound, which extended from the end of his nose to his forehead.

But it would be a short break: Roadrunner had set up a full year of touring. On August 19, the band were scheduled to go out on the road with the gothic gloomsters Coal Chamber and the San Francisco neo-thrash outfit Machine Head, both of which were at that point vastly more successful than Slipknot. The dates were labelled the "Livin' La Vida Loco Tour", a snide reference to the similarly-titled, nauseatingly plastic Ricky Martin hit single of the time.

Apart from tales of the unprecedented live antics of the band, it wasn't long before reports of Slipknot's unusual on-the-road rituals soon began to filter through to the press. One of the more legendary stories included the presence on stage of a large glass jar, which Corey would carry on with him and which excited a huge amount of curiosity. It contained a brownish, huddled lump which was unidentifiable even in close-up. Ultimately it was revealed that the strange matter was in fact the decaying corpse of a crow – a *spiritual* crow, according to the band. Corey started opening the jar

mid-show, sniffing deeply of its odour and vomiting into the crowd. It has been said that fans would vomit in response, and even that he would catch the contents of his stomach in a container and throw it into the moshpit, many of whom would 'upchuck' in response. Not your usual on-tour tales, then: it's not surprising that the public's attention was becoming more and more focused on the band.

Eventually the unfortunate crow became little more than a foul-smelling soup, with the jar a nest of maggots. Too appalling even for Slipknot, the end came when some teenage fans grabbed the jar after a show, emptied it onto the floor and started kicking the semi-liquid contents around. However, there were plenty of other repulsive things for the band to do: one famous example came to pass when Shawn and Corey were approached by a policeman at an Iowa concert. He had a gift for them: a severed beaver tail. Barely in control of themselves, the drummer and singer started chewing bits of the tail and spitting them at each other:

fluids dripped from the revolting piece of flesh and it was ultimately torn to shreds. Laughing manically, the two finished the set, but when they came offstage and regained a measure of sanity, they ran to the toilet and threw up for hours.

Before embarking on the Livin' La Vida Loco tour, Slipknot played Mancow's Lazer Luau, an all-day festival on July 31. Fulfilling the highly satisfying role of local boys made good, the band put on a crushing show. Their performance of 'Wait And Bleed' was filmed as part of an MTV video and also became a bonus track on the enhanced 'Spit It Out' digipack single, released in April 2000. It's a malevolent, uncompromising rendition: Corey introduces the song with the words "Are you ready to take this fuckin' place apart? Let's fuckin' do it – this is 'Wait And Bleed'." The crowd are ecstatic, even at this early stage in the band's new-found popularity: Slipknot respond to this with a performance of almost suicidal commitment.

SID WILSON
MEETS HIS PUBLIC

Sid and Shawn physically attack each other onstage, Joey bangs his head like a maniac and the guitarists are bent over so far, their masks are almost touching the stage. Word that this was a band of almost terrifying power spread rapidly.

The band wandered about maskless and relished the opportunity to enter their audience unobserved, as Joey told *Kerrang!*'s Robyn Doreian: "After the show, the fact that I can walk through a bunch of people and they are all standing around talking about the show, and I walk by and they don't even know it's me, or that I'm in the band. If that is one of the downfalls, then it is the best downfall

The frenzied in-store session was now typical of the reaction that Slipknot were getting from their fans. Sales of the album had rocketed, helped along by the band's mighty performances on the Coal Chamber/ Machine Head tour. It was on this tour, for example, that Corey introduced one of the most memorable routines of the set: as 'Spit It Out' began, he would ask the crowd to kneel or sit on the floor of the venue. "Don't get up until I say get the fuck up!" he would warn, and sing the first couple of verses before giving the command: the room, of course, tended to go insane at this point – the sight and sound of several

"You might have a lot of money and be famous, but the next time you talk shit about Slipknot and its fans, we will kill you." COREY

I have ever heard of because I get to hear the kids talk and they don't even know who the fuck I am, and the fact that they say such kind words about us is such a good feeling."

August saw another bizarre incident in the increasingly surreal world of Slipknot. Visiting the town of Norridge, Illinois for an in-store signing, the nine members of the band were putting on their jumpsuits and masks in the car park when they were approached and challenged by police officers. The cops apparently thought that the band were robbers en route to a nearby jeweller's store which they planned to hold up. Compelling them to stay on the pavement, the police began to interrogate the band: after a few minutes it became clear that Slipknot were not about to steal anything and the situation was resolved with some merriment. In fact, the officers remained at the scene and watched the band meet hundreds of fans at the store, Rolling Stone Records. The signing took over three hours.

hundred metal fans leaping to their feet is memorable, to say the least. At the end of September came the welcome news that *Slipknot* had gone gold in the US – that is, had sold over 500,000 copies nationwide. On the Montreal date of the tour, the news came that the album had also gone gold in Canada. Roadrunner were astonished: this made the album the label's most successful debut ever. It was an awesome achievement: after all, metal, despite its diverse forms, is still not reckoned to be a contender in sales terms compared to the Mariah Careys, Puff Daddies and Celine Dions of this world. Metal neither commands the granny pound nor the kiddie pound, two fearsome market forces at this time. And yet this weird-looking band from the middle of nowhere had sold a gold record in less than three months – and a twisted, agonised record at that. Furthermore, this took no account of export sales: in territories such as Germany, Britain and Scandinavia, where sales figures were similarly

healthy. And all without the benefit of a chart single or mainstream exposure. Something quite unusual was clearly afoot.

Slipknot's rise to notoriety was confirmed when other bands started slagging them off. Fred Durst, frontman of the now enormously successful rap-metal outfit Limp Bizkit, had allegedly passed some uncomplimentary observations about the band in an interview. Getting wind of Durst's comments, Corey made some similarly provocative remarks about Limp Bizkit at a show in Dallas with Machine Head on October 31. This has spiralled into an ongoing feud between the two bands, with too many insults exchanged to detail, but one of the choicest episodes concerned Durst's alleged comment that Slipknot's fans are "fat, ugly kids" and Slipknot's subsequent offer to fight him and his band – except for Bizkit guitarist Wes Borland, who enjoys Slipknot's respect for some undefined reason. Corey is said to have made the following remark about Fred at a Knot gig, "You might have a lot of money and be famous, but the next time you talk shit about Slipknot and its fans, we will kill you."

Both press and fans love all this, of course, and it shows no sign of ending: it's been demonstrated that such rivalries only enhance public awareness of the protagonists. Many fans also enjoy the combative sense of taking sides, which makes the dispute all the more attention-grabbing. In Slipknot's case the situation is exacerbated by the fact that both they and Limp Bizkit have fallen out with Korn, the other member of the Big Three of Nu-Metal.

One of the more unpredictable swings on the erratic Slipknot merry-go-round took place when they were asked to appear on the New York shock jock Howard Stern's radio show. Stern was taken aback by the band's demeanour, which – I kid you not – started with Shawn's unusual decision to defecate in a nearby fire bucket, which he then handed to Stern as a souvenir.

After the mostly small-venue tour – which allowed the fans to witness the Slipknot experience at close, almost Safari Club-like quarters – and a short break, Slipknot spent some time discussing the Purity Knight issue with Roadrunner. The album was duly reissued in December. Two years on, it seems that little notice was taken of the move: the fans have discussed the whole unsettling saga so many times that the internet chat rooms are no longer full of Purity rumours and the issue has become part of the ever-more-bizarre Slipknot mythology.

Slipknot had other important things to think about, anyway. A 44-date world tour was looming, spanning three months, with in-store appearances and press duties for every show: it was a major undertaking by anyone's standards, especially for family men such as Shawn Crahan.

December 1999 saw Slipknot on the front cover of the UK metal magazine *Terrorizer* and playing at London's Astoria as part of *Kerrang!*'s X-Fest shows on the 13th. British metal fans had welcomed Slipknot, who returned the favour by playing in the UK several times in the next year. After a Christmas break Slipknot regrouped and began the tour, which set off on January 18 in Atlanta, Georgia and included more dates on the next five nights in North Carolina, South Carolina, Virginia and Washington DC. The venues were medium-sized, and mostly full to the brim: most of the United States knew by now who Slipknot were and wanted to see the evidence for themselves. Slipknot had taken two uncompromising support acts with them, Will Haven, a multifaceted metal act with its own quirky charm, and Kittie, a brand-new all-female act from Canada with a ruthless onstage routine.

The date in Oklahoma in late January was a disaster. The venue was packed to the gills and before the show could start, a local fire marshal decided that safety standards had been compromised. He is then alleged to have asked the tour management to eject 60 members of the audience to make the

event safer, although why fewer tickets weren't made available to prevent this situation is a moot point. Slipknot refused point blank to ask the fans to leave, but the official remained adamant. The band then refused to play and left the building; an announcement was made that the show would not continue and the crowd became angry, uprooting fixtures and destroying much of the venue. The blame goes to the inefficiency of those who organised the ticketing allocation. The concert was later played on February 22, with all tickets from the earlier date still valid.

The madness continued, with the Washington show on January 23 marked by controversy. Halfway through the Slipknot set, Corey suddenly held aloft a copy of a popular teenage magazine. The pages he displayed to the crowd were an advertising spread for Calvin Klein, the American clothes manufacturer. The model in the picture was none other than David Silveria, drummer with Korn. Silveria, a muscular, athletic man with model-like looks, had been asked to pose for the ad, which had invoked Taylor's wrath as a sign of bowing to the corporate machine. Allegedly shouting to his audience that Korn were "sell-outs", Corey then lit the magazine and threw the burning pile of paper to the stage, where Shawn then stamped on it. The fans went wild, cheering them on. When reports broke internationally, metal fans were divided – after all, Korn and Slipknot both represent the same style of music, give or take a few thematic and musical variations – until Korn singer Jonathan Davis publicly stated that he agreed with Slipknot's action. The other members of Korn were also unhappy with Silveria's decision to model, he said, and there was no disagreement between the bands on the subject.

The mini-festival tour then moved on with shows in Pittsburgh, Grand Rapids (said to be a 'dead town' rather like Des Moines) and three shows in the Canadian cities of London, Toronto and Montreal. There was

then a six-day break while the band left Kittie and Will Haven behind to fly to that cash cow of world tours – Japan. Three dates in Tokyo and Osaka were scheduled for the first week of February. Another three-day rest would take place while Slipknot moved on to Australia, taking in all the major cities on an east-to-west trip: Brisbane, Sydney, Melbourne, Adelaide and Perth.

And so the Slipknot tour rumbled on, with a stop in the US in late February before testing the uncharted waters of Europe. February 25 saw a performance on NBC's popular *Late Night With Conan O'Brien* TV show, with a suitably telegenic performance of 'Wait And Bleed', which had been earmarked as the band's first single. The band then embarked on the February-March UK tour, which proved to be the band's most dramatic to date. Shows were scheduled for Nottingham Rock City (February 26), Glasgow Barrowlands (28), Manchester Academy (29), Wolverhampton Civic Hall (March 1), Portsmouth Guildhall (3), Bristol Anson Rooms (4) and London Brixton Academy (5).

The first date, at the veteran metal venue Rock City in Nottingham, went down a storm. The British music press had been salivating at the thought of witnessing Slipknot on their own ground and were suitably impressed by the band's onstage aggression. Interviews by Joey, Shawn, Corey and the band as a whole appeared in the music press as well as the mainstream newspapers, both tabloid and broadsheet – a departure for the British media. All seemed to be going smoothly until February 27, the day before Slipknot were set to play at Glasgow's elegantly-decaying Barrowlands Ballroom. The band were booked to do a series of in-store signing sessions at HMV stores, starting that day at the Glasgow branch. However, at the last moment the branch's management decided to cancel the session, to much outcry. A spokesperson for the store made a public statement: "We turned them down because their popularity

has risen tremendously. Our concern is that so many fans are going to turn up – there would be in excess of 1,000 people. We are concerned about everybody's safety: both the safety of our staff and the safety of our customers." HMV's high-street rivals Virgin rapidly stepped into the gap and offered to host the sessions at their Megastores, with the Glasgow session allocated for the following day. Band and management agreed and the in-store appearances duly took place, with hundreds of albums sold and little reported discomfort: the schedule was booked as Glasgow (February 28), Manchester (29), Birmingham (March 1), Portsmouth (3) and London Oxford Street (5).

On February 28, the three-track 'Wait And Bleed' digipack single was released, containing the Terry Date Remix of the title track (a brighter version than the album original, with Corey's vocal cleaner and more prominent in the mix – Date is a well-known metal producer who had worked with old-school thrashers Dark Angel, among others, in the Eighties), the very appositely-titled Overcaffeinated Hyper Version of 'Spit It Out' (again more crisp than Sean McMahon's recording, with what sounds like an extra vocal harmony from Corey and lots more percussive sample sounds) and the Molt-Injected Mix of '(Sic)' (a version not radically different from the mighty album track, other than a slightly more radio-friendly overall texture). It also contained the alarmingly committed video footage of Slipknot performing 'Wait And Bleed' back home in Iowa. The band were both relieved and disgusted to hear that MTV was playing the 'Wait' video several times a day. The station, which remains the definitive music television medium by virtue of its incredible viewing figures, has become regarded as something of a slick, commercial environment by the increasing number of bands whose music contains a specific (or otherwise) anti-corporate message. But they still need it...

The mayhem didn't stop there. The next day, after an ecstatically-received show in Glasgow, the fears of the HMV spokesperson came to fruition when over 1,000 fans turned up at the Manchester Virgin Megastore for the Slipknot signing. Like their counterparts in Glasgow, HMV in Manchester had – wisely, as it turned out –

also refused to host the session, allowing its more adventurous rival to take the plunge. The disruption was so extreme that the entire city centre was jammed for some time.

Things couldn't get any crazier, many observers thought. But they were wrong. On March 1, the Slipknot bus rolled into Wolverhampton. The gig had briefly been in jeopardy some months before, when word had reached the musicians – at the time, ensconced at home in Iowa – that the local Conservative council wasn't happy at the

of his heart-stoppingly spectacular stunts by leaping off the thirty foot high first-floor balcony into the crowd. Wilson managed to climb onto the ledge, having come around the backstage area and up the stairs, and without pausing to think, flung himself outwards and backwards, with his arms stretched out in a crucifix position and his black gas mask waving in the air. Had the crowd suddenly parted, as occasionally happens, there is no doubt that he would have been seriously injured or killed: as it

> "I don't think that some of this band's actions are quite the thing we want at our Civic Hall, which is owned by the council. They would not find this band acceptable at all." BRITISH CITY COUNCILLOR

booking. One of the councillors had stated that Slipknot were "not welcome at all" and had described them as "ridiculous, juvenile and stupid", and was alleged to have said: "I know I'm old and a fuddy-duddy, but I don't think that some of this band's actions are quite the thing we want at our Civic Hall, which is owned by the council. As a representative of the people of Wolverhampton, I can say that they would not find this band acceptable at all. I'm quite broad-minded, but one has to speak as one finds."

Joey's response was predictably outraged. "I'm going to shit in a box and send it to Wolverhampton council!" he vowed. "We'll see how acceptable they find that. Anyway, I'm sure I can bribe some of these councillors with poker money I've won in our dressing room." The whole episode went down as one of the more surreal of Slipknot's brief history. During the concert at the Civic Hall, DJ Sid Wilson decided to perform one

happened, his fall was broken by a 19-year-old girl called Lyndsey Pearce. She was knocked unconscious and was carried away by medics. She soon woke up, dazed and concussed but not injured.

Speaking to the press the following day, Lyndsey was remarkably reasonable about the whole episode, evincing no ill-will or resentment to Sid or the band. In fact, she insisted that the show was 'the greatest gig ever'. "I broke my glasses and so could see even less when I came around," she remarked, before adding, "but on the other hand, I had also attended the greatest gig ever!" She even felt honoured by the attention bestowed on her. "Everyone treated me really well, including the medics, Slipknot's tour manager and Sid," she pointed out. Wilson, it seems, is less deranged and more caring than his appearance would indicate. "He came to see me and was really concerned. He began to cry, and I just melted," said Lyndsey. The final word on the

matter has to be her conclusion that, "The truth is – Slipknot were everything I expected them to be."

In publicity terms, probably the biggest stroke of luck on this tour was Slipknot's landing of a live spot on the popular Friday evening TV show *TFI Friday*, hosted by the DJ Chris Evans. This took place live on March 3 at the show's Hammersmith Riverside studios before the band travelled to Portsmouth for a concert at the city's Guildhall. Surprisingly, the performance of 'Wait And Bleed' went smoothly, with no unduly coarse language from Corey. Evans had built up the appearance in previous shows by airing footage of the band's 'Wait' video: the response from viewers and the live audience was remarkable, with a whole new demographic – the dance / hip-hop nightclub/wine-bar crowd – made aware of Slipknot. Whoever was responsible for organising publicity appearances for the band on their 2000 UK tour had their finest hour on that evening, with literally millions catching their first glimpse of the Knot.

After a farewell show at London's Brixton Academy on March 5, Slipknot departed British shores for an altogether more peaceful set of dates on mainland Europe. The tour took in shows in Holland, Belgium, France, Spain and Italy, and all went smoothly until March 21, when four days after a show in Madrid, and the day before the tour was to resume with a concert in Vienna, the band unexpectedly announced that the remaining seven dates of the tour would have to be cancelled. The official explanation was that 'personal issues at home' were affecting one of the band members and that refunds would be given for all tickets. The exact nature of the unidentified player's problem has still not been revealed, but Slipknot have repeatedly said that without even one member, the band is not the full band. It's not surprising, therefore, that they chose to cancel the rest of the tour rather than continue with a man down.

In April the 'Spit It Out' single was released. This was packaged as a red vinyl seven-inch or an enhanced CD: the former had a live version of 'Surfacing' on the B-side, while the CD also contained 'Wait And Bleed' live and the video clip made for 'Spit It Out'. This was an entertaining parody of the famous Stanley Kubrick film *The Shining*, and had recently been banned by MTV on grounds that it was too violent. Standout scenes include the diminutive Joey playing the part of Danny, the son of Jack Nicholson's psychotic hotel caretaker, riding a four-wheel pedal car around the spooky corridors of the Outlook Hotel; Corey re-enacting the "Here's Johnny!" moment in which Jack sticks his head through the wood of a smashed door; and James fending him off with a baseball bat.

More film footage had been shot for the first Slipknot video release, a 20-minute documentary-cum-performance video which had been compiled by Roadrunner from interviews, live films and various items such as the 'Spit' promo clip. Titled *Welcome To Our Neighborhood*, the band were astounded to learn in June that it had jumped straight to the top of the *Billboard* charts. To tie in with the release, Slipknot put in a guest appearance once more on *Late Night With Conan O'Brien*. Another high point for Slipknot occurred in June, when the band played a show with Iron Maiden at the Eindhoven festival in Holland. "Iron Maiden are the gods of metal!" said Joey, never slow to pay respect to the old school when it is due. They also played at the Dynamo show at Nijmegen, where Corey addressed the crowd with the words "Welcome to the year of Slipknot, Dynamo!"

The world of music was disturbed in the early summer of 2000 by the news that the music website Napster was in the process of being sued by the San Francisco band Metallica, whose drummer Lars Ulrich made a series of high-profile appeals to the US court handling the case. Joey, interviewed by the UK news and music website nme.com, said: "Metallica are one of the biggest rock

bands in the goddamn world, so what the hell would they need to sue Napster for? It is retarded," before referring to Metallica's much-criticised crossover from thrash metal to rock with the words, "Why don't they practise their fucking job and see if they can still play like they used to, not this new

incorporate it for themselves. Where stores close at 9:00, the internet is open 24 hours a day. Record labels need to wake up, take control of it, and realise that it's the future of music because there's no stopping it. I do not condone people when they are ripping off art, period. So as far as MP3 today –

lame crap. That's what I am more concerned with." He also discussed the possibility of releasing some or all of the follow-up to Slipknot via the internet, pointing out that "What bands need to realise is that it will always be more fun to go and buy a CD with the booklet and information take it home to listen to... the cheapskate assholes who aren't that much into music are going to [download songs from the internet], but I'll buy a CD every time."

Shawn had an opinion, too, telling *Loudsides*: "The internet is a wonderful, wonderful tool, but everyone needs to wake the fuck up and take it by storm. And what's happening is that MP3s are so massive and so revolutionary that record labels need to take it under fire right now and learn how to

I fucking hate it, but as soon as people get their shit together and they can come up with a system and it's locked down, then it can become a good thing, but until then it's not."

Joey's statement was made on June 29, 2000 – one year after the release of *Slipknot*. What a year it had been: the contrast between the Slipknot of 2000 and that of 1999 was marked. Experience had taught the band much, although they knew that they were still at the bottom of a steep learning curve. Year on year, the band's environment had slowly but steadily become more and more surreal. Widespread success had only illuminated this all the more. What lay ahead, therefore, was likely to be stranger still.

CHAPTER TEN

2000-2001

By this stage in the remarkable story of Slipknot, the band had risen to the top of the metal tree, overshadowed by a mere handful of bands. Korn were as big, but lacked the unique cachet that being the current hot band of the day confers; Iron Maiden commanded a larger audience and wider respect, but only after two solid decades of activity; the once-underground Metallica were now a cultural phenomenon, but had exchanged the respect of die-hard metal fans for mainstream chart blandness. Other than these, however, no other metal band had climbed as high or as rapidly as Slipknot.

However you analyse the secret of their success – shock tactics, songwriting talent, the visceral live shows – their reputation was consolidated once they'd reached the top by one other important factor: their newsworthiness. Slipknot set unprecedented standards by penetrating beyond the usual music media and appearing in broadsheet newspapers worldwide. This ubiquity was self-supporting, and the more they showed up in print, the more convinced the world's press were that they should continue to do so.

Perhaps the ultimate sign of the band's penetration was that fans could now buy the famously 'anonymous' Slipknot jumpsuits from the Blue Grape merchandising company – and don't think the irony of this was lost on more astute observers. Equipment manufacturers had also taken note of the Knot presence – Mick, for example, signed an endorsement deal with the guitar maker BC Rich and uses their Warlock instruments, which along with the Jackson Custom has been the thinking metaller's preferred axe for several years.

The next major platform for Slipknot was the prestigious headline slot at the 14-date Tattoo The Earth festival, a travelling multi-stage show along the lines of the Ozzfest – the 2000 version of which ran concurrently – which began on July 14 in Portland, Oregon. The increased profile of metal in previous years had tied in with its new Nineties image – piercings, make-up and body art – and the idea of a festival made up of stages and tattoo tents made perfect sense to the thousands of fans who attended, plus the organisers, who even released a TTE compilation album, *The First Crusade*, late

in 2000. It was a prestigious tour: the regular line-up of performers included top-end outfits such as Slayer (who were the second act after the Knot), Coal Chamber and Sepultura, mid-range acts like Nashville Pussy, Puya, (hed) pe and Downset and new or new-ish upstarts such as Hatebreed, Full Devil Jacket, Famous, Esham and Mudvayne, with whom Shawn Crahan had worked and who went on to be something of a nu-metal phenomenon in their own right. The first gig saw a one-off appearance by Stone Temple Pilots, while the TTE schedule also included a stop at the New York Giants Stadium in New Jersey, where the headliners were none other than Metallica. All this was a long way from the previous year's Ozzfest, which Slipknot had opened. But at that time, of course, they hadn't sold many albums. The total at this stage of Tattoo The Earth? Over a million, making *Slipknot* platinum plus.

The full schedule was Portland, Oregon (July 14), Lawrence, Kansas (18), New York (20), Scarnton, Pennsylvania (21), Boston (22), Cleveland (24), a welcome homecoming to the Waterworks Park in Des Moines (27), Somerset, Wisconsin (28), Milwaukee (29), Pontiac, Michigan (30), San Antonio, Texas (August 2), Mercedes, Texas (4), Houston (5) and Dallas (6). The programme was intensive for the bands – and equally so for the promoters, who had to organise the construction and breakdown of the enormous stages and tents in a matter of hours – but at least the musicians had a day off from time to time.

The tour was, of course, not unmarked by controversy. A classic Slipknot escapade occurred at the Wisconsin show, where Shawn, the band Hatebreed, a Slipknot drum technician and a couple of members of One Minute Silence were involved in a fight with the over-zealous backstage security. Shawn and some of the others were driving a golf cart around the closed-off area – the image of a nu-metal Elvis (who also used one of these laughable vehicles) is a hard one to shake off – and spotting him trundling past,

a security officer asked him to stop. The reason the security man later gave was that he was afraid for the safety of the concert-goers. Whether or not this was the case, the consequence was that Crahan disagreed and was pulled off the cart by the security guard and a couple of his colleagues. Not unreasonably, Shawn objected to this treatment and a fight began. Members of Hatebreed and related tour personnel, all friends of Crahan's, saw what was happening and waded in and – just like a Western saloon-bar brawl – within seconds everybody was punching everybody else. Hefty as Crahan is, and tough as Hatebreed undoubtedly are, the security guards were professional bouncers and rapidly overpowered the musicians, giving Crahan a dose of Mace for good measure. Both parties filed police reports, but no charges were brought and that, it appears, was that.

The British metal magazine *Kerrang!* played a large part in the promotion of Slipknot in the latter part of the year. Its annual awards ceremony was to take place on August 29, just three weeks after the close of the Tattoo The Earth concerts, and rumour had it that the band were to be nominated in various categories. The magazine had taken the band to its bosom, interviewing them before the New York gig with Metallica and producing a special magazine in their honour, which detailed the band's past, profiled its members and featured interviews from associated honorary Knot members such as Ross Robinson. In one interview, Shawn indicated that when preparing for the follow-up to the *Slipknot* album, the band would try to re-create the conditions in which the first had been created. His parents were prepared to move out of their house and give the band the old basement where they had spent so many years honing their songs, he said. Perhaps more bizarrely, he claimed that Corey had asked for his old job back at the Des Moines porn store where he had spent many evenings writing song lyrics. Not for Slipknot the plush rehearsal suites

and pre-production budgets of many rock stars. Just as so many other publications had done before it, *Kerrang!* also inquired about the causes of Slipknot's ever-present rage: this time it was Joey who provided an answer, and it's perhaps the clearest explanation which has been provided to date. "When you receive the amount of ridicule that we did from our hometown," he said, "and when you get that middle finger as often as we did – you just want to throw it back in their faces."

However, before the *Kerrang!* awards could take place, there was another landmark appearance for Slipknot to make. They were booked to play on the main stage at the British Reading and Leeds festivals, which after the annual Glastonbury mega-festival are the country's most publicised. The gigs – one in each city – took place on August 25, 26 and 27. Slipknot played third on the bill on different days – one in each city after Stereophonics and Placebo (Joey later said that these two bands literally sent him to sleep). The bands who performed before Slipknot were My Vitriol, Supersuckers, A, Daphne & Celeste – a clean-cut teenage duo who had been added as an ironic gesture by the organisers towards the largely metallic bands on the bill – the brat-punk band Blink 182 and the mighty Rage Against The Machine. Jordison later admitted that he had felt uncomfortable playing ahead of RATM, who had laid down the original template for Slipknot's early rap-metal. He was right to feel that way – respect was due, as without RATM there would have been little or no nu-metal, the genre into which Slipknot partially belongs. The respect is mutual, though: Rage guitarist Tom Morello said: "I think that Slipknot is awesome. It's just so furiously over the top. A friend of mine went to see them, and he gave a review of them that I think was one of the best reviews of a band I've heard in a long, long time; he was like, 'I feared the drums, man. I feared the drums'. And when you've got someone fearing the drums, you know that you're doing the right thing." Another band with

close ties to Slipknot is Amen, who opened for them at two dates in October.

The Slipknot performances were intense, disciplined sets, designed to counteract the rather off-putting fact that the show was in broad daylight (many bands complain that in the harsh light of day, they find it hard to perform to their best) and to impress the Slipknot message on a new group of fans: the British festival crowd, who, while no strangers to metal (Reading in particular was always an old-school rock-fest) had not been exposed to metal-oriented festival bills to the same degree as their American counterparts. Festivals dedicated to metal are common in Europe (Wacken, Eindhoven, Dynamo) and the US (Ozzfest, Warped, Milwaukee Metalfest, November To Dismember) but any attempt to organise a similar event in the UK has not been successful since the mellowing-out of the once-legendary Castle Donington show which ruled the roost in the Eighties. In playing the Reading and Leeds gigs, Slipknot exploited a powerful opportunity to expose their music to more mainstream rock and pop fans, as the major acts at the show included Oasis, Primal Scream, Foo Fighters and their old friends Limp Bizkit on the first day and Pulp, Beck and Deftones on the second.

The *Kerrang!* awards came and went, leaving Slipknot with no fewer than three awards and a ratcheted-up reputation for sheer boisterousness. The magazine and its readers voted Slipknot Best International Live Act and Best Band In The World, as well as awarding 'Wait And Bleed' a gong for Single Of The Year. Overjoyed, the band set about creating as much havoc as possible, setting fire to their table and overturning it, smashing glasses, microphones and chairs and starting a food fight. This last insanity left food lying all over the venue, so much so that the actress Britt Ekland, who was presenting an award, slipped on a piece of watermelon and was carried to and from the podium with a broken ankle. Other awards went to Stereophonics (bet that woke Joey up),

Deftones and Queens Of The Stone Age, who coincidentally grew up in a nearby town to Ross Robinson. Pictures of the event show a bizarre scene: the evening took place in the dining-room of a top London hotel, and it's strange to see the band in jumpsuits and masks, destroying everything they can get their hands on. By now Shawn had cut the hair off his clown mask, leaving a bald, smooth pate, having claimed that it had "gotten nappy" after the months of abuse it had endured.

Juvenile as these actions may seem, more serious stuff was to come. The day after the awards ceremony, Slipknot were scheduled to fly to Dublin for a gig that night at the well-known Point venue. Arriving in Dublin, the band and tour management were informed that the show had been cancelled due to 'logistic problems'. This immediately sounded implausible and on further investigation, it was discovered that an independent pressure group, the National Parents Council Of Ireland, had formally objected to the show, although it was never officially stated that this was in any way responsible for the concert's cancellation. A spokesman for the NPCO confirmed to the press that an objection had been made to the promoters, MCD, because of the supposedly 'obscene' nature of the Slipknot show. The idea that the concert would be offensive or disturbing had been exacerbated by the band's appearance in a local newspaper: the spokesman added that he had received several offensive messages, presumably from disgruntled fans.

In mid-September Joey was quoted by several news sources as having said, "We were banned because the parents over there think we're going to warp the kids' minds. And we would have, too." A more considered statement than it appears at first, his words sum up the situation quite succinctly. Of course the violent Slipknot show isn't going to 'warp' anybody — but it might well open the fans' eyes to things which, rightly or wrongly, aren't thought to be appropriate. The issue of Slipknot as a cause for parental

alarm is difficult to resolve. They swear a lot, it's true, and they occasionally urinate on each other on stage. Add to this the sometimes gruesome lyrics and the odd smutty — and harmless — gesture such as Chris performing jerk-off motions on his nose, stir in the genuinely awe-inspiring live spectacle and the power of the band's music and the result is inevitably a cause of worry for many a protective adult. And so it should be, for parents of children of a certain age. But what some authorities, parents among them, fail to recognise is that for the majority of children — even in their very early teens — the school playground and extended social sphere is one enormous barrage of so-called 'bad' language, shockingly new experiences and — unfortunately — a certain amount of violence, whether witnessed in others or endured at first hand. In a situation such as the cancelled Dublin concert, it is for parents to make an individual decision based on their own values, the way they perceive the concept of an 'upbringing' and the personality of their child. If the gig was cancelled as a result of moral pressure — and I must stress, this was never officially said to be the case — then it remains a typical example of an ill-thought-out, knee-jerk reaction, and the metal fans of Dublin are the worse off for it. Far be it from me to moralise or judge — but common sense must prevail when assessing an issue such as this. And in this case, it may have failed to do so.

On September 16, Slipknot appeared on the cover of the *NME*, in which Shawn spoke about the band's roots and the psychology of their music. With the warning "I am a fucking threat. I am an extreme threat," Crahan gave a surreal interview, telling a story about a schoolboy who had nicknamed himself Frayed Knot (a play on "I'm afraid not") and who had committed suicide. His teacher later wrote to Roadrunner, thanking Slipknot for adding some colour to the boy's life. He ruminated that "inevitably" he would ultimately retire from public view, perhaps on an island or up

a mountain, "so I can't bother people and they can't bother me". Life in Slipknot could be extremely dangerous, he said, detailing an on-stage incident in which he and Wilson were urinating on each other, unaware that the streams of fluid were falling perilously close to some high-powered strobe lights concealed under Joey's drum riser. Had the urine touched the lights, it would have meant instant death for one or both men. He also described himself as "30 and overweight", and still performing backflips despite two permanently broken ribs and express medical advice not to do so.

Joey wasn't short of a choice anecdote, either. He recounted how he had recently approached Limp Bizkit's DJ Lethal – who had allegedly called Slipknot "a boy band made of WWF guys" and said, "You suck, I don't like your band, you stand for everything I'm against", and challenged him to physical combat, which the Bizkit decksman declined. Despite this unlikely macho front – Joey is normally a peaceful, even cerebral person – he came across well, showing an appreciation of the current music scene and putting on a subtler act than the more confrontational Crahan.

September 2000 was a belligerent month for the rock world, it seems. On September 17 the US punk band Green Day played at the Virgin Megastore on Oxford Street in London for fans only. A member of the audience threw a clown mask on stage, which singer Billy Joe Armstrong picked up and put on with the mocking words "We're Slipknot, fuck you". He then threw it back into the crowd, contemptuously snarling, "Oh *scary*, you've got masks, assholes. Why don't you try writing a good fucking song for a change?" Towards the end of the set his banter between two songs included the charming words, "Dedicate this song to the person you hate most in the world. Think about killing the bastard. Take Slipknot, for instance." Armstrong was clearly on a roll, also aiming jibes at Metallica and Blink 182. Punk, eh? It's isn't known if Slipknot have ever dignified this tirade with a response.

Four days later, yet more news broke with the announcement that a series of gigs scheduled for the rest of the month had been cancelled, due to the physical exhaustion and/or illness of a member of the band, who has never been named. Doctor's orders were to rest and refrain from touring after the musician fell ill at Los Angeles airport. The incident was remarkably similar to the previous string of cancellations prompted by the 'problems at home' of one of the musicians in March, in that the party was not identified and no concrete reason was given. Still, it's to be expected: with the Slipknot shows such a physical workout for the band, and given the packed schedule which they are required to fulfil, it isn't surprising that cracks have started to appear: they are not – as Shawn's broken ribs testify – made of iron. Crahan even said in the *NME* interview that it was probable that one of them would die on-stage at some point – although how serious he was about this is a moot point.

After some days off, Slipknot played ten shows in Washington, Boston, New York and Philadelphia, between the end of October and the start of November. All nine men seemed to be on fine form and, whatever form the mysterious illness had taken, it had obviously been surmounted.

And so the band continued. The awards mounted up: Ross Robinson was a nominee for the Best Producer award at the yearly Q Awards on October 16. The prize eventually went to Robbie Williams producers Chris Power and Guy Williams, but the short list was a select one – Dr Dre was one of them – which indicates the penetration of the Slipknot message. In January 2001 'Wait And Bleed' was nominated for a Grammy for 'Best Metal Performance' – a giant leap forward for a band as specialised as Slipknot. On hearing the news, Corey responded with the following, somewhat bizarre speech: "In the 5th century BC, there was a Samurai warrior who had an interesting way of celebrating his birthday. Every year, he had what he called his 'Resurrection Day', where he would give himself a new name, possibly to become another person. He did this every year, taking a new name and living his life as if that would be the last year he was alive, which in theory was correct. The parable here is that you never know what is going to happen as your life goes on. This year, Slipknot is nominated for a Grammy, which I consider a great honour. But you never know what's gonna happen next year. My heart is thrilled that we've even been considered for this. And at the same time, my brain tells me to be happy, but never, ever be content. For content is the death of dreams. And we've got

a lot of dreaming left in us." Pretentious? Maybe. Eccentric? Definitely.

Crahan commented on the nomination with the words, "To be nominated, it's unbelievable, it's unbelievable that the kids are getting the recognition. Because really, if you think about it, they're really the ones blowing Slipknot down everyone. The kids, the maggots, are the ones telling their parents, 'Hey, I've finally got something that's helping me through the day.' It's the kids who request us on MTV, who won't play us, and it's the kids who got us into the Grammys, into their heads. To think that anyone involved in anything as big as the Grammys took the time to spell out the word 'Slipknot' is an extreme honour for me and the band, we have known the work that we've put forth to this world, and we're very, very intense about what we do. Being nominated for Best Performance is an extreme honour, because that's the way we live our lives: 190 per cent. For the industry to recognize that and to say our name and actually give us the nomination makes each one of us in the band feel like what we're doing is making a change, and that's what we set out to do from the very beginning."

A sign of the band's confidence and, dare we whisper it, stability, has been the emergence of various members' side projects. One of the most talked-about in 2000 was Corey's solo album, which he described as "more hard rock than metal" and which was recorded with Sean McMahon back at SR Audio in Des Moines. In a classic wheel-coming-full-circle situation, guest vocals on one track were handled by none other than Anders Colsefni, while the drums on the album – tentatively titled *Superego: Click Here To Enter* – were handled by Painface drummer Danny Spain. Another track, 'Weight', is said to include eight singers – Corey, Shawn Crahan and his son Gage, Aaron Peltz (Painface manager), Jim Corigliano (a mamber of the Des Moines band Heroic Dose), Sa-Tone (Shawn's drum technician) and Dizzy Draztik (the singer of

Jordison's side project, The Rejects, who were in the process of signing a deal with Roadrunner at the time). Sid Wilson has also landed himself a solo record deal with 1500 Records under the name DJ Starscream, while Shawn, too, has his own project under construction.

On November 5, 2000, an album of songs by the hardcore punk group Snot was released in honour of its late singer, Lynn Strait, who had been killed in a car accident. Titled *Strait Up*, it attracted a host of metal and punk names, including Serj Tankian of System of A Down, Korn's Jonathan Davis, Max Cavalera of Soulfly, Ozzy Osbourne, Fred Durst and Corey, who performed vocals on a song called 'Requiem'. It was acknowledged by the participants that Snot would have been one of the next bands to break into the big time and that the loss of the young Strait was a particularly tragic event. Culturally, the album represented an unprecedented coming-together; musically, it was remarkable to witness the Big Three Of Nu-Metal (Korn, Bizkit, Knot) on a record together. Corey also put in a superb cameo on Soulfly's second album, *Back To The Primitive*, released in December 2000. He duetted on 'Jumpdafuckup', a mass of bass-heavy riffing and monstrous vocals by the leather-tonsilled Max Cavalera, who also recruited artists as diverse as Slayer's Tom Araya and Sean Lennon to guest on other tracks.

The year 2000 was brought to a close, appropriately enough, with a front cover for Shawn Crahan on the Christmas issue of *Kerrang!* It was the first sighting of his new, 'improved' – i.e. more unsettling – clown mask. The old one had finally bitten the dust after almost two decades of wear, and the new version was much scarier, with realistic-looking veins, a detectably more demonic expression and a row of inverted, reddened screws in the shape of a mohican haircut. Asked how he felt about the state of the music business, he growled, "I'm just pissed at the industry, the industry can suck my ass." On the subject of the new album, however,

Crahan was more upbeat: "This new album is going to shut people up because if you thought you knew what Slipknot was about, you have no idea, because we're not that new band any more."

His mood would have cleared, it can be assumed, after a Yuletide break: on January 17, 2001, Slipknot entered LA's Sound City studios, again in the capable hands of Ross Robinson, to record album number three (although various members of the band refer to it as the second, ignoring *MFKR* completely or categorising it as a demo only). Robinson called the pre-production "smoking" and "pure molten metal". The new record was beginning to sound like something of a landmark. The Slipknot obsession with extreme metal had not faded an iota, for starters: Mick was asked to join the death metal band Brutality in 1999 – but declined politely – and Slipknot had even perfected a cover of Terrorizer's 'Fear Napalm'. Joey promised *Terrorizer* in 1999 that the next album would begin with "full-on blastbeats and black metal screams", and told *MetalUpdate* "Wait till you hear our fuckin' next record. It smokes our first album. The shit's twice as technical, three times as heavy. The first track on the album's gonna be called 'People=Shit'. It opens up with a grindbeat with sixteenth-note double-bass and four layers of black metal and death metal screams."

But the Knot were still popular outside extreme metal. Marilyn Manson asked Joey to take the master tapes of his January 2001 single, 'The Fight Song', into SR Audio for a remix, where he added drum parts and lengthened the song, describing it as "like a Hell's Angel in the front row at a Slayer gig". It was released on January 29. Joey also appeared briefly in the video for Manson's cover of Soft Cell's 'Tainted Love' shortly after.

Everybody loved Slipknot at this point, it seemed. But then they hadn't heard the most extreme work of their career – and in the summer of 2001, the next album was unleashed.

CHAPTER ELEVEN

2001–2002

The media doesn't miss many opportunities to exploit any marketable image, and conclusive proof of Slipknot's entry into mainstream awareness came when the band was asked in spring 2001 to make a cameo appearance in John McTiernan's remake of the 1975 movie *Rollerball*, a cult action classic in which a future society is depicted getting its kicks from the sight of roller-skating sportsmen maiming each other in the name of entertainment. The band appeared for a few seconds performing a new song from their forthcoming album – a move which acted as a teaser for both fans of the movie and the band. "We as a band are excited to be part of this movie," Slipknot said through their press office. "We are big fans of the original and we know the new version will be much better." Their involvement added a touch of unpredictability to the expectation building around the movie, which (like so many remakes) was predicted both to be a triumph and an unmitigated disaster. For the results of their anticipation, fans would have to wait until August.

The announcement also finally came that Slipknot's second major-label album would be released on June 19, 2001, and that a five-date warm-up tour would be played in April in America's Midwest, although not in the band's home state – all the more ironic as the record's title was revealed to be (simply enough) *Iowa*. As soon as the name was announced, online chatrooms burst into a frenzy of speculation, with fans asking each other what Slipknot meant by it: was it a tribute, or a vilification, of the state which had caused them so much sorrow? Would they be abandoning their home town, or returning to it as conquering heroes? However, all this brainstorming was fruitless, with little clarification coming from Slipknot themselves, who appeared to be going through a mildly chaotic period at the time: no sooner had the warm-up tour and album release been scheduled, for example, than a statement came from them that a postponement on both counts was necessary. The tour was cancelled entirely and the album release delayed until July 17 – the reason they gave was that extra time was needed to complete the final mixes.

However, a series of European tours would be taking place after the album's appearance, it was announced, with an October tour with System Of A Down also in place, to be titled the Pledge Of Allegiance Tour (this title would gain a certain added undertone, of course, due to events which would occur just weeks before it started rolling).

All this confusion added enormously to the build-up to *Iowa*, of course, helped along by Corey, who told *Rolling Stone* in April that the band was looking forward to heading back out on the road: "We've got a little bit of money behind us now, so we can branch out," he mused. "I'm not sure exactly what's going to be used [in the stage set] but it's going to be a lot of steel, a lot of hydraulics. It's going to be dangerous. Everybody in the audience is probably going to be thankful that they're not onstage." Apocalyptic words indeed: fans asked themselves exactly how extreme the Knot's show could be, after all the live excesses of before. An interesting point was Corey's revelation that Slipknot now had some financial muscle to wield, indicating that some at least of the significant revenue from the *Slipknot* album had been reinvested in the live show: clearly there was a business brain or two among the nine members and their management.

It all began to make a kind of twisted sense when *Iowa* finally appeared, even later than had been expected, on August 28, 2001. It had been preceded by a one-track promo CD of a track called 'The Heretic Anthem' in a simple white card sleeve featuring a detail of a goat's horn: the song was a blistering slice of near-death metal and was much heavier even than Slipknot's previously most brutal work, 'Sic', and didn't get much radio airplay accordingly, although expectation levels for the album were heightened among fans thanks to its wholly new degree of power. Even extreme metal fans who would normally not approach supposedly nu-metal bands such as Slipknot were impressed; although the sound of 'The Heretic Anthem' was recognisably Slipknot, Robinson's bass-

heavy production had taken the song to a deeper, more crushing level, while Corey's familiar growl had been honed and hoarsened by constant touring to give a pure bellow of which death metal vocalists such as Deicide's Glen Benton would be proud. This was clearly a whole new band: and Slipknot's followers queued up to buy *Iowa* with a mixture of excitement and trepidation.

Although *Slipknot* had been a dark, heavy album, *Iowa* fulfilled the promises of Joey, Corey and Shawn by destroying it utterly. A multi-layered album with an almost orchestral degree of complexity and many strata of sounds, it utterly levelled the chart competition (which in that particular week included among its ranks Staind's second album, *Break The Cycle*) and extended the remit of nu-metal by being harsher and angrier than any previous record from the genre. It immediately sold in huge quantities, and entered the UK albums chart at No. 1 – an achievement which even those who had predicted that it would make a huge impact had failed to foresee. *Terrorizer* magazine (a bastion of extreme metal which suffered few poseurs, whether in the name of metal or otherwise) stated a few weeks after its release that *Iowa* had become the "biggest-selling extreme metal album ever made".

Right from the off it seemed that *Iowa*'s central purpose was to reaffirm Slipknot's roots in extreme metal, and thereby redefine nu-metal. Its cover (on both the CD and double-vinyl formats) was a garish silver portrait of a goat's head (the quintessential black metal icon since the early-Eighties satanic days of Mercyful Fate and Venom, and replicated endlessly in the following decade by the Scandinavian underground), and the chorus of 'The Heretic Anthem' had been notable for its reported shriek of "If you're 555 [the fictional area telephone code used in Hollywood movies], I'm 666 [the Biblical number of the beast]".

Joey made his feelings clear about Iowa's extreme metal roots when he was asked by *Metal Edge* if the album represented "Slipknot

going death metal". He said: "No, we're not 'going' that, we've always *been* that. The thing is, I don't want to limit ourselves to that specific genre because we're all into various different types of music. In order for us to get the music out that we want, or the music that we want to create, we want to bring something new and not rehash shit. That's why we have nine guys in the band, because that's what it took to get us the sound that we wanted and the sound that we were craving, and that sound is *not* death metal or black metal. But we're lumped in with a

for the city of Des Moines. Instead of Corey's high-pitched gabble of "The whole thing I think is sick", however, this time the vocals are simply a collage of screams, with only the word "Death!" being identifiable at times. It's a more venomous band this time around, and no mistake: an impression bolstered by the fearsome heaviness of the much-discussed opening track, 'People=Shit', which Joey had talked up all those months before as a pure death/black metal hybrid. This is certainly true of its opening minute or so, a pure slab of grindcore reminiscent of resolutely

bunch of bands right now, because of our success, that we really don't feel like we have anything in common with musically. This album is about making an about-face from all the other bands, to fucking get away from that whole genre of music. This is more of a 'revenge' album to the nay-sayers that saying that we're pure metal or whatever. It wasn't done as a conscious effort, it's just what flew out."

Like its predecessor, *Iowa* began with a disturbing, electronic composition from Sid Wilson and Craig Jones, this time called '[515]', another area code reference, this time

extreme acts such as Cryptopsy, Gorguts or even *Domination*-era Morbid Angel, those Jordison heroes. This section of the song is a carefully-constructed arrangement of blastbeats, roars and a downtuned riff from Root and Thompson which puts all other nu-metal axemen to shame: it's followed by a more melodic structure with a shoutalong chorus, true, but for a moment there 'People=Shit' is the heaviest piece of music ever committed to tape by a nu-metal act, with no exceptions. And we're only on track 2...

The next song, 'Disasterpiece', is less of an onslaught than 'People...', and is based on a

standard, scratchy riff reminiscent of 'Surfacing', although its bridge accelerates to thrash velocity for a bar or two: it's a brief pause for respite before 'My Plague', which takes Slipknot into new territory. Destined to be the second single from the album, 'Plague' has a bizarre, ice-cold chorus reminiscent of Fear Factory, whose reverbed, chilling anthems were an uneasy presence through Nineties metal. It also contains a staccato, technical section which Slipknot could have lifted directly from a progressive metal album such as Metallica's 1987 classic *Master Of Puppets*: it's not the kind of song which leaves the listener feeling relaxed or complete, ending with a seething flourish of industrial sounds.

Which is only appropriate, as it is followed by Slipknot's sickest song to date: 'Everything Ends', in which vocalist Taylor exorcises the pain of a broken heart in the most agonised way possible. It seems that a relationship has ended: "Everything I see reminds me of her/God I wish I didn't care anymore", he spits, in apparently genuine pain – before the first chorus of "You are wrong, fucked and over-rated/I think I'm gonna be sick and it's your fault" he almost inaudibly gasps "Fuck!". What makes this song so weirdly appealing – and strangely, for most fans it remains merely an album track, without much discussion attached to it – is the atypical way in which it deals with the thorny subject of love. Slipknot are lovers as well as fighters, it seems, but deal with it in their own way – with anger, vengeance and honesty. It's a tough listen.

'Everything Ends' is succeeded by 'The Heretic Anthem', an almost lighthearted song after all the angst which has gone before it. Counted in by an electronic voice (which slyly runs "10... 9... 8... 7... 6... 6... 6... 5..."), it's a melodic song affirming Slipknot's alienation from their environment – although there's a creeping sense as the album progresses that the band have named their best work to date *Iowa* because the ethos of that state is actually a part of who they are:

the grimness of Des Moines, the city which they have so often reviled, runs through their veins. Iowa is a part of Slipknot, and Slipknot is irrevocably a part of Iowa.

This being Slipknot, there has to be room for a chilling, horror-movie song in their repertoire, and this time it is a re-recording of 'Gently' from *Mate. Feed. Kill. Repeat*, which had originally been a vehicle for Anders Colsefni's shape-shifting *Rage*-derived lyrics: in Corey's hands the song is more ambiguous. However, it's the combination of guitars and metallic ambience in the first few minutes of the song which make it what it is: effectively it's a horrifying instrumental with some shouted lyrics at the end, and a numbing experience.

The mood changes subtly with 'Left Behind', a more obviously commercial song (although don't expect an easy listen) which would be the first single from *Iowa*. It's based on a slimy, almost snakelike riff and a chorus which startled many fans by its sheer catchiness. "As I close my eyes" and "We all got left behind" are the lines which stick in the head, both based on a rapid arpeggio which Corey sings in his 'normal' (i.e. non-bellowed) voice, reminding the listener that he can be a superb conventional singer when he wants to be. "We let it all slip away" harks directly back to the image of the slashed-wrist suicide awaiting death in 'Wait And Bleed', and in some ways the songs are parallel – both are more melodic than the rest of the songs on their respective albums, both were released as singles and both are difficult to forget. For many Knot fans 'Left Behind' was the finest song they have ever written.

But just as the album is taking shape, Slipknot surprise us all with a change of direction. With the obvious chart appeal of the two singles, the almost human tone of 'Everything Ends' and the fist-punching extremity of 'People=Shit', *Iowa* sets out its stall as a finely-honed, exactly-defined record – but its second half is darker and much more vague, leaving the listener feeling

slightly sick (perhaps a part of the band's intention). 'The Shape' contains more spooky echoes along the lines of 'My Plague' and takes an almost prog-rock-like step into a new tempo, with a variety of unexpected riff changes, after a deceptively simple opening section. 'I Am Hated' is its evil twin, a song which is hard to pin down or classify: there are death metal complexities in the structure, but an almost catchy element to the arrangement which creates an overall impression that the song is just plain *wrong*.

'Skin Ticket' is even weirder, a cacophonic soup of Paul Gray's almost jig-like bass, jammed, scraped guitar wails and Joey's cymbal-heavy percussion. It's difficult to get inside the song: Corey starts off with some insane laughter, before whispering some certifiable lyrics in an almost Jonathan Davis-confessional style against an unpredictable

backing. Of 'Shape', 'Hated' and 'Ticket', it's this last song which is the strangest and most unsettling – almost as if Slipknot are mocking their own expertly-crafted work on the first half of the record and throwing in some gut-churning horror just to keep the listener uneasy and awake.

And then there is a brief semblance of a return to normality with 'New Abortion', which despite its grim title is a fairly conventionally-structured song along the lines of 'Purity' or 'Left Behind'. Not that it's easy listening: it's heavier than anything on *Iowa* apart from 'People=Shit' or 'The Heretic Anthem', and does contain its fair share of unbalanced sickness thanks to some Robinson-processed vocals and a dash of ambient noise from the always-present Jones, whose malevolent noise-injections make so much of Slipknot's sound recognisably their own.

'Metabolic' is more of the same not-quite-normal, but-more-normal-than-'The Shape'

material which spirals the record down into the ultimate horror of its final track, which gives its title to the album. An ascending, unhinged riff underpins the song and brings the listener gasping to the opening of 'Iowa', which is actually a remake of 'Killers Are Quiet', another track from *Mate. Feed, Kill. Repeat*, which had helped to give that album such a disturbing tone. It's a long, trancelike ride to the end of the record, and at over 15 minutes in length is the perfect vehicle for Corey's brooding thoughts (he can be heard panting, laughing, snarling, whispering and chanting at various points), allowing Joey and Paul's metronomic rhythms to anchor the whole composition, Ross Robinson to experiment with the studio tools at his disposal and for the band as a whole to improvise with atmospheres. Its final 30 seconds are a barely detectable sub-bass drone as the sound decays, topped off with some kind of evil electronic rattle. It's a horror movie in sound, and the darkest work that any mainstream band has produced in the new century.

With *Iowa*, Slipknot came home. Although their two previous albums had been open, variform and innovative, their third was the work of a band at that crucial juncture – the point where songwriting and performing experience has reached masterful levels but has not yet quenched the hunger and the need to self-express. The emotions of *Iowa* are (in order of frequency) anger, desolation, glee and despair, all of which reveal themselves in the textures of the music and the images (rather than the actual words) used in Corey Taylor's lyrics. Aided by Robinson's sympathetic but never lax production (remember, this is the man who said "Take it back... make it fucking sick" to both Corey and Jonathan Davis), the band created a monster in *Iowa* and named it after themselves in a masterstroke of introspection.

As always, the band put equal focus on the visual side of the project. As they were no longer the new boys on the block, Roadrunner had allocated a significant post-production budget to *Iowa*, enabling a silver card booklet to be used (one side of which was actually a mirror, forcing the *Iowa* message – whatever each listener decided that should be – onto everyone who picked it up). The jewel case contained an image of a goat foetus beneath the CD and the interior of the booklet folded out into a long transparent sheet. This was no mere "album" as such: it was a cultural and musical event.

So what does it all mean? What are we to infer from all the anger and the negativity that *Iowa* bestows on us? Perhaps simply that there is beauty in anguish and ugliness, and that horror can lead ultimately to redemption. After all, the members of Slipknot are broadly normal people, as we have seen – and maybe the pain which they broadcast via their records is nothing more than normal. Perhaps their nightmare belongs to the rest of us, too? The metal-buying population of the world certainly thought so, and the album was an enormous commercial success despite the near-unplayability of so many of its songs.

The Slipknot-featuring remake of *Rollerball* was also released in the summer. As so often occurs with remakes, it received very negative reviews on its release on August 17, with critics pointing to the misguided casting (the callow Chris "*American Pie*" Klein was no substitute for the original hard-bitten James Caan, and support slots by LL Cool J and Jean Reno were deemed too lightweight and a waste of a great talent, respectively) and the lack of any real need to re-enact the movie in the first place. Luckily, the Slipknot segment was an entertaining performance piece in which the band were allowed to demonstrate their full on-stage madness (albeit in suitable-for-TV format) and had no real connection with the rest of the film.

Iowa continued to sell well and receive plenty of cable-TV exposure (MTV had taken the Knot to its bosom) throughout the events of September 11 and beyond, although Roadrunner did not release the 'Left Behind' single until 29 October 2001, when the

novelty value of an album as brutal as *Iowa* topping the charts had given way to mainstream acceptance that it was simply a solid, popular record. The single's almost unstoppably catchy chorus-line paid off in spades, helped immensely by the deeply disturbing video which accompanied it and which was almost constantly played (in full or edited format) by many music channels worldwide.

The video was set in the depths of a Midwestern forest and saw the nine-piece performing the song in a clearing in the woods, with Shawn and Chris alternately elevating on their new extendable drum risers and the rest of the band placed at intervals. A flock of sinister-looking goats roamed between the players (I interviewed Joey shortly afterwards, who told me that one of them jumped onto Shawn's drum riser and attempted to butt him). In this video Crahan was also showcasing the third phase of his clown mask, a completely reconstructed, nightmarish visage with the clown nose and grin replaced by a miserable frown, a pentagram etched into the face and segments of the head removed to show the sides of a realistic-looking brain. Cut between the footage of the band performing the song is a narrative in which a pale-faced teenager goes to work at a butcher's shop, where his task is to cut up a horrible-looking piece of offal – a task he completes with glassy-eyed enthusiasm, to the suspicious stares of the butcher and his customers.

A storm is brewing both in Slipknot's forest and in the desolate town where the meat-cutting kid lives, and as events intensify (he goes home, pours brown liquid from the tap into his plastic-looking cereal and settles to watch TV – only to have a rock thrown through his window by some mistrustful children), the weather begins to worsen. In the forest, Joey, Mick, James and Paul are attacking their instruments, Corey and Shawn are adopting a kind of sickened crucifix posture and Chris is masturbating his nose (if you go down to the woods today, eh?) as the rain

comes down in sheets. Finally, the child's TV explodes on the last note of the song, he runs into the forest, opens a door set into the ground and vanishes inside it – whether on his way to hell, to a state of metaphorical isolation or to death, is not revealed.

Quite simply, the 'Left Behind' video was a masterpiece – the teenagers who followed Slipknot loved the way it spoke to them of alienation and withdrawal, while fans of any grimly gothic art admired its dark undertones and its subtle, censorship-dodging imagery. It had been intended to accompany the band's twenty-four-city US tour in support of *Iowa*, and would in fact have made a suitable movie accompaniment to the spectacle of Slipknot on the road, had not a sudden development meant that all their plans had to be relaid. Shawn Crahan's wife Chantal had been diagnosed with Crohn's Disease, a serious intestinal ailment which required surgery and extended treatment: this meant that the entire tour was postponed until early 2002 until she was capable of looking after the Crahans' three children again. European dates had been scheduled for the early months of 2002 and were unaffected.

As if to continue the message of dedication to extreme metal, Slipknot invited the Swedish death metal band In Flames to tour with them on these 2002 dates. This was an interesting and controversial decision, and one which was another step in the move towards the mainstream of extreme metal which had been in progress since the late Nineties. For example, the successful Texas metal band Pantera had invited the resolutely underground Norwegian black metallers Satyricon to tour with them in 2000★.

Initially, however, many extreme metal fans were dismayed that a band such as In Flames (which, as one of the pioneers of the New Wave Of Swedish Death Metal [NWOSDM], were held in great respect by the underground) would elect to tour with a 'chart-metal' band like Slipknot. In Flames frontman Anders Friden countered the ensuing allegations of sell-out, explaining

how the unlikely pairing came to pass: "We met Slipknot in Italy a couple of years ago," he said. "We just started talking and some of them said they were fans of our music. We were kind of surprised. We never thought that they would know about us." Of course, since the early days all the members of Slipknot except Sid Wilson (a self-confessed rave junkie) had been patiently explaining to the press how much they loved death and black metal, but it took a respected death metaller like Friden to make people listen: "Some of [Slipknot] are huge metal fans in general," he explained. "They're all cool, all nine of them." The audiences had given IF a great reception, he added, not

camera angles of the songs you wanna see. We did this with 26 different cameras. We just went above and beyond to make this the best DVD possible."

Paul Gray was also enthusiastic about the DVD, informing MTV: "We wore these little microphone pin cameras, so [the viewer will] be able to click on whatever band member and watch from that guy's point of view," he said. "But it was a pain in the ass because they gave us this big [camera] pack that we had to wear around our waist. So when I was jumping around, the thing started sliding down my leg. I managed about four songs with that thing before I ripped it off. And Sid, he jumped out in the crowd and

"They're all cool, all nine of them."

without a slightly underhand allusion to what is metal and what is not: "I guess the people enjoy a real metal band. They see us up there working really hard for half an hour and I think people can appreciate that. It's doing really good for us. Getting us out to a lot more people who haven't heard us before. It's kind of a dream come true".

The tour sold out and was an unmitigated success, with the new, tougher sound of Slipknot welcomed by European audiences, who also enjoyed the Rage Against The Machine-alike riffing of second support act American Head Charge. The February show at London's Wembley Arena was especially anarchic, with Sid flinging himself into the audience and being returned with his overalls ripped almost to pieces and without his camera. A DVD was later released of the show, and received rave reviews: "The DVD's gonna be fucking amazing," Corey told *Rolling Stone*. "I've seen the footage for it and it's fucking fantastic.
It's gonna have everything, man – it's gonna have all our videos that various stations won't play [and] some backstage stuff. There's gonna be special features where you can change the

they ripped his coveralls completely off and stole the camera. We ended up getting it back and all that's on the film, which is pretty cool." His memories of the UK tour also extended as far as the last show there, which had taken place in Birmingham and turned into sheer chaos: "All the kids started ripping off the seat covers from all the seats, so about half-way through the set there were about 8,000 seats being thrown around," he said. "We had this big seat fight with the kids in the crowd. Then, since it was our last show, all our techs started beaning us with eggs, so we had this nasty mayonnaise and eggs and ketchup food fight."

After a couple of months of recuperation, mid-2002 saw an entirely new development from the Slipknot camp. It appeared that not only had some of the band gone back to their roots, but the decision which fans had thought would never be made had in fact already been taken. It was with some shock that fans switched on their TVs in the summer to hear that two Knot side projects were up and running – but this time, with a difference.

This time, the masks had come off.

CHAPTER TWELVE

2003 & Beyond

I *owa* had caused ripples everywhere, it seemed, with most reviewers either cowed by its malevolence or celebrating its uncompromising power. But Slipknot weren't planning to rest on their laurels: Joey even reported that the band had started work on their next record. "It's pretty fucking brutal still," he said bullishly. "If you like 'People=Shit', you're gonna like our new stuff. Slipknot has the Slayer mentality: you know exactly what you're getting into when you buy our fucking record."

He elaborated a little for the benefit of those who thought his band had reached the limits of recorded aggression and would surely implode if the music got any harder: "The thing with this band is it's so extreme, and it's so special, and it's something you can't keep recreating over and over," he explained. "We're not a formulated band. We have our certain thing that we do. Each album is a progression from the last – something's heavier, or there's something a little more twisted or atmospheric about the new one than the last. But there's gonna be a limit to how far we can go with it. It might be two more albums, maybe three, maybe one, I don't know."

Although it had become a cliché to say so, Slipknot was now something of an unstoppable machine, with product emerging every few months irrespective of whether the band were actually creating anything new. The *Pledge Of Allegiance* album appeared in late 2001, containing songs recorded live onstage by the Knot and their touring partners System Of A Down, the Armenian-American quartet from LA who had been making almost as many waves in the nu-metal world as the Iowans. In fact, it's fair to say that SOAD changed the face of metal just as much as Slipknot in the period from 1998 to 2002, investing the slightly stale nu-metal format with a quirkiness derived from the traditional Eastern European melodies which they used in their work and their decidedly skewed world-view.

After you've appeared in a film, another sign of increased commercial kudos in American showbiz has to be the appearance on a movie soundtrack of your music – and in March 2002 the *Resident Evil* soundtrack was released to accompany the film based on the popular Playstation game of the same title. Starring Milla Jovovich, the movie

(actually a fairly lacklustre futuristic slasher pic) reveals much about the state of mind of American youth (or the 'Prozac Generation', as media analysts were calling them), whose slacker interests made such a film – a combination of pure horror, shoot-'em-up gore and nu-metal – the perfect entertainment. The soundtrack included songs by Coal Chamber, Fear Factory, Mudvayne, the Crystal Method, Depeche Mode and Ill Niño, as well as Marilyn Manson's Jordison-tweaked remix of 'The Fight Song' and Slipknot's new single, 'My Plague', which was subtitled 'New Abuse Mix'. The song had been rejigged by Limp Bizkit/Deftones producer Terry Date and included cleaner vocals and some refocusing of the arrangements. Bassist Paul Gray explained of the remix to MTV that the idea had been to make the song radio-playable: "On the album version there were some kind of weird vocal effects on some of the parts, and we took them out and just had Corey sing," he said. "Also, we had to do some editing in the middle because there's a part that goes 'Kill you, fuck you, I will never be you' and with the movie coming, they wanted to be able to use the song on radio."

A sell-out? Probably not in practice: as Gray went on to explain, the reasoning behind creating a 'clean' version of the song was based on artistic integrity, not for simple cash-flow purposes: "You can sit there and listen to a Jay-Z song on the radio, and half the lyrics are cut out," he pointed out. "So we mixed it up and changed it so our song wouldn't be all cut up and shitty-sounding." This makes sense – and in fact the audible gaps in a simpler, censored radio mix might have been construed as a deliberate ploy to gain attention through shock value.

The normally taciturn Gray also had a lot to say on the subject of the new album, pointing out that the new material would have a more complex edge than their previous work: "We've got a bunch of different riffs together," he said. "Some are really heavy and some are more technical.

We want to get tighter with the songwriting. Everybody has their own version of what should happen, so when we get in the studio we're gonna take everybody's different ideas and try to make them blend smoothly." Interestingly, it seems that he felt that Slipknot's songwriting – already sharp as a razor – could be improved upon; and also that certain people still saw the Knot as less-than-gifted players: "Since we're a lot heavier than Linkin Park, a lot of people think they're better musicians than us, but we can play just as fuckin' well," he observed, apparently apropos of nothing. "We're gonna write [stuff] that will maybe shut up a few of the people who don't think we can actually play."

After contributing the Molt-Injected Mix of '[Sic]' to a NASCAR racing-themed compilation album called *Crank It Up* (the Knot song was a highlight alongside Slayer's slightly bizarre cover of Steppenwolf's 'Born To Be Wild'), Slipknot encountered their unlikeliest adversaries to date in May 2002 in the shape of the Knitting & Crochet Guild, an English organisation with about 1,000 mostly female members interested in embroidery and other harmless needlework tasks. The controversy arose when a group of British Knot fans found on the internet that the title of the Guild's quarterly newsletter was entitled *Slipknot*, so named after the initial loop made when beginning to knit a new garment.

The magazine, founded in 1978, contained little to offend anyone – let alone nu-metal fans – but this particular group of Knot followers seemingly took offence at its name and bombarded the Guild with obscene e-mails and even phone calls. The membership secretary, an understandably bemused woman called Anne Budworth, was quoted as saying: "I don't know how anyone could confuse us with them. I haven't ever seen the band knitting," and, reasoning that perhaps the fans had been irked because the official Slipknot website was not functioning: "Some of their fans were irate, but obviously if the Slipknot site is down, it's not our fault, is it?"

Rita Taylor, the chairwoman of the Guild, remarked, with some justification: "There is no need for this kind of thing. It is quite offensive. We would like to make it quite clear we are nothing to do with this group. Some of the messages we have received from Slipknot fans have been very unpleasant." Despite the offence caused, the incident soon passed into Slipknot's history as one of the more surreal episodes that the band had endured.

It was at about this time that rumours began to spread that the band were working on new material which would involve the removal of their masks. Sid Wilson was the first to do so when he played a set at the UK's Gatecrasher dance event in Northamptonshire in June, which saw him – with only a bandana covering his face – perform a mixture of ear-bleeding drum'n'bass tunes to a mostly speechless crowd. A Roadrunner spokeswoman pointed out beforehand that: "Sid's a massive drum'n'bass fan and a serious DJ, so it makes sense for him to play at Gatecrasher. He often does these sort of things and he's looking forward to it".

However, concrete announcements that some of the members would appear in public fully unmasked finally came with the revelation that not one but two new Knot-related bands would be stepping into the limelight in the summer of 2002. The first was none other than Stone Sour, the band in which Corey Taylor and James Root had played before joining Slipknot: the Des Moines quintet had signed a deal with Roadrunner and would be releasing a self-titled album in August, featuring Sid on three tracks. A video for a single entitled 'Get Inside' had been shot at the Whisky A Go-Go in West Hollywood, which would feature both men close up without masks.

The publicists were as good as their word. When 'Get Inside' was released, the video went into immediate heavy rotation on most music TV channels: it was a standard performance clip with much focusing on the faces of Taylor and Root, who were revealed to be entirely normal-looking men. The former denied that SS was any sort of Slipknot substitute, saying: "As soon as this mask comes off, it's not Slipknot anymore" – a statement backed up by the song 'Bother', on which he sang with an almost wistful delivery and which was scheduled to appear on the *Spider-Man* soundtrack. "If you're in a band, why do another band that sounds the same as the other band?" Taylor added. "Branch out and do something different. There are things in this band that I can't do in Slipknot. And if I can't do them, I'll lose my mind."

Stone Sour (which Corey confirmed was named after a cocktail) consists of guitarist Josh Rand, bassist Shawn Economaki (also Slipknot's stage manager) and drummer Joel Ekman. The reformation had come about after Rand met Taylor in 2000 and told him that he had some new songs: the pair regrouped and the rest fell into place rapidly. Corey revealed that some of Slipknot's fans had been a little confused by this development: "I've gotten a lot of questions from kids asking me if I'm going to wear the mask onstage, and I'm like, no, what are you talking about?" he said. "I'm not going to make [Stone Sour] Slipknot Jr. As much as I love Slipknot, I don't want that to carry over into what I do for Stone Sour. I want both bands to stand on their own."

But there *was* more to Stone Sour than met the eye. As Corey told *Rolling Stone* writer Anthony Bozza, the band needed to happen: "I was really getting burnt out with what I was doing with Slipknot," he said. "I needed to get back to where I came from – melodic singing, more stripped-down kind of music – and this was the perfect time to do it… This was about branching out and doing a whole different type of music. If I had to go right into another Slipknot album, I wouldn't have been happy. I wouldn't have been able to put my whole heart and soul into it, and it would have sucked. So this was basically me showing the world I can do

more than just fucking scream and punch myself in the head".

The collaboration fell together very easily, as he explained: "Me and Josh have known each other since we were sixteen and we've been writing stuff on four-track for years," Taylor said. "I had just got back from Japan, and he came over with the blueprints of what basically became 'Get Inside'. We just started writing stuff and it started to happen. We ended up writing 14 songs and going into the studio and doing demos and basically looking at each other and saying, 'Man! You know what? I think we're going to have to put a real band together, because this is just too serious!'"

Simultaneously, Joey Jordison had renamed his side project The Rejects, calling them The Murderdolls and recruiting Static-X guitarist Tripp Eisen into the ranks. They had also signed to Roadrunner and an album, *Beyond The Valley Of The Murderdolls*, was distributed to press at the same time as Stone Sour. Joey – who had moved to guitar for the new band – had removed his mask to reveal his pale, slightly pinched features. As for the Rejects' music, it was a beefed-up mixture of hair-metal anthems with freaky, Marilyn Manson-esque themes – song titles on the album included 'B-Movie Scream Queen' and 'She Was A Teenage Zombie'. Weird stuff – but designed, said Taylor, to allow the band-members a little time to reflect on the work of their main band: "It's good for us to go out and do stuff," he explained, "so when we come back to Slipknot, we'll once again discover why we love it in the first place."

Wise words, and it seems certain that the musicians will return to Slipknot in due course – to their home band, where they need to be, and where they should be: and that is the end of their story for the moment.

But before we say goodbye to Slipknot, let's allow the eternal wheel to come back round and return us to where we started – Des Moines. It hasn't received a very good press in this book, and yet when you look at it in the bright light of day, away from the festering psychological horrors of the Slipknot members' minds, it's just another city. A little quieter and less adventurous than many urban areas, perhaps, but ultimately still a place where people live and work and die. How has it changed – or *been* changed – since the unexpected success of its least favourite sons? Let's ask Mike Lawyer...

What was the Des Moines public's initial reaction to Slipknot?

"Very mixed. But there hasn't been – as far as I'm aware – any outcry from any religious organisations or conservative factions. The biggest reaction has been because of what it's done for the musicians and the musical scene. There still isn't a musical scene in terms of venues to play in, there's just a few places. But what's happened since Slipknot has broken out – and this is great for recording studios and great for me – is that because musicians don't have tremendous numbers of places to play, they're writing and recording all the time. They play in Omaha, they play in Kansas City, they play in clubs in Minneapolis and St. Paul."

Why do you think they've made it so big?

"Well, the band are absolute workaholics, especially the core members Shawn Crahan and Joey Jordison. They are the ones who hold that band together. Shawn is just as intense as everybody else, but he's a family man, he's got good business sense and he's still one of the original founders with Paul."

Do the fans like the fact that they're so aggressive?

"Hmm. I don't want to spoil their image, but what was interesting was the way they played that up in the press. Maybe they were asked to play up the fact that they are these aggressive people. But then later on I started reading in some of the European press that after a couple of incidents – some stage-diving where people got injured and things like that – it toned down a little bit. As if they were saying, we're just performing on stage, we don't cut the heads off goats when we're home. And it's true. To hang out with

the guys on a one-to-one level, they're really great guys. Corey Taylor really loves his grandmother and she has gone out on the road with them on the Ozzfest! But you're never going to read a story like that in the press. Corey's grandmother's standing at the side of the stage at the Ozzfest with a laminate on, while Corey's out there screaming 'Motherfucker!' at everybody. And she was proud of him, too. So there's that other side to them, but when they're on stage they're 150% Slipknot."

They're willing to bleed and kill themselves on stage further than most, and when you see them it's like, whoa! Most bands hit it 90%. Slipknot hit it *exactly* the way it is on the record."

But perhaps it should be left to Shawn Crahan, who started it all off, to summarise the effect of being in Slipknot, as he did in the *Des Moines Register*: "It's a hard thing for your own mother and father to tell you they've read interviews and look you in the eye, and they wonder what they've spawned,"

JOEY AND COREY

As for Kyle Munson? He writes, with typical professional objectiveness, as follows: "Success means that Des Moines is suddenly under scrutiny as an unlikely birthplace for this latest, most extreme brand of metal. These children of the corn are a homespun tale of not-so-ordinary madness."

Slipknot's old friend Ross Robinson looks back with great affection at their last two years. When I asked him if he was surprised at the heights they have reached, he replied tranquilly: "You know what? The depths that that band give of themselves, I'm not surprised at all. They live it, breathe it, everything, there's no holds barred.

he said. "What they've spawned is the real deal. I believe I've been put here for a purpose." He also evidenced some annoyance at the negative effects of Slipknot's success, telling *Loudsides*: "Now I look back and all the bands in Des Moines want to be heavy. They all got DJs and samplers and they're all caught up in image. It's sick, dude. It's pathetic."

Despite these angry words, he seems to have developed a more relaxed attitude, perhaps, in recent times, and appreciates what he has achieved, saying in *Kerrang!*, "The last two years turned out slightly different to how I planned, but they've been pretty exciting."

To say the least... He also knows that the Slipknot recipe is not to everyone's taste: "You either love us or you hate us. Get over it!" As for their feelings towards Des Moines, perhaps a truce has been struck at last – the *Register* again: *Crahan says he's proud of his Des Moines origins, but the harsh winters and his desire to indulge in various artistic side projects makes the prospect of a move more likely. Sid Wilson, however, is about to purchase a house on the city's east side. He's smitten with his home.* "*I love Des Moines,*" *he says.* "*I don't care if the whole band moves somewhere else, I'm going to be in Des Moines.*"

Perhaps the rage that the band have always displayed towards their home town is just one half of a love-hate relationship – always the most destructive kind. Even back in July 1999, Crahan had told the journalist Bushman of the Seattlesquare.com webzine that his roots would always be in Iowa: "I am not ashamed of where I'm from. Never will be. Y'know, I'll probably live there the rest of my life. It's quiet, it's my mentality. I can focus on my dreams and who I need to be there. I don't have to pretend to be anything. I've got no pressure from anybody. Record label people don't like to come there. Record industry people don't like to come there. And we don't want them there anyway, man. We want to fucking write music and we want to write it our way and we don't want any help and that's the way it goes. So we're all good man, I'll probably live there the rest of my life." Even Ross Robinson is aware of this gentler side of the clown: "He'll learn to ease up. It's a lot to take because they got so huge all at once. He seems to be someplace else, but his heart is pure and beautiful."

So what can the future hold for this band? Can the next album equal the mighty *Iowa*? If it does, it will be a mighty beast indeed, and just one more reason to be a metal fan in the early years of the third millennium. However, nothing is for certain: Crahan had the following words for *Sweet Suffering* when asked how he saw the band's future: "This band is not going to last. I have three kids and a wife, and I don't want to leave them. That would be against what we are. We have plenty of years left in us, we have plenty albums out there, plenty good shows and songs, but the minute the whole world gets Slipknot, then we're done... I just want to be left alone for the rest of my life, with the people that I love the most. I wanna fish and grow tomatoes, and watch my grandkids! And sometimes sit with the guys from the band, and talk about these old good times. Because they *are* good times, I love them all, it's a surreal dream that surrounds us. But it's going faster than we can do it, and there is a time when we'll have to put an end to it."

Whether or not his words are prophetic will only be revealed as the years pass. And even if Slipknot can keep up this furious pace, who knows if the music will remain as good and as powerful as it has been to date? Not even the band know that.

However, the wider issue is not about the quality of the band's music. It hinges on Slipknot's relationship with society, and whether they can co-exist. After all, we've seen as many people try to hinder Slipknot as have followed in their wake: they are, as Crahan has put it, a band that inspires love and hate in equal measure.

But it's not about liking Slipknot. It's about accepting them for what they are. Don't blame Slipknot on society – we *are* society. Don't bother to look for the causes of their anger – we *are* those causes. The modern world created Slipknot, and the modern world has to accept that responsibility. Which, of course, includes *you*.

In the final analysis, we all love, we all hate, and we all push against the world we live in. But we don't show this on our faces. No: we all wear masks – our search for an identity is one of the goals we set ourselves. Some of us even find it.

We are all part of Slipknot, and Slipknot is a part of every one of us. Or, as Shawn Crahan put it: "There's no getting rid of us. We're the virus that there's no cure for. Because we're the virus that *is* the cure."

DISCOGRAPHY

SINGLES

WAIT AND BLEED (Terry Date Mix)
SPIT IT OUT
(Overcaffeinated Hyper Version)
[SIC] (Molt-Injected Mix)
Roadrunner RR 2112-5
(enhanced CD, digipack, includes
"Wait And Bleed" live video);
February 2000

SPIT IT OUT
SURFACING (Live)
WAIT AND BLEED (Live)
Roadrunner RR 2090-3 (CD);
April 2000

LEFT BEHIND
LIBERATE (Live)
SURFACING (Live)
LEFT BEHIND (Video)
Roadrunner RR 23203355 (CD):
October 2001

MY PLAGUE (New Abuse Mix)
HERETIC ANTHEM (Live)
SIC (Live)
MY PLAGUE (New Abuse Mix)
(Video)
Roadrunner RR 20453 (CD):
July 2002

CDs

MATE. FEED. KILL. REPEAT
Ismist - ISM CD 742617000027
(US only, 1000 copies);
July 1997

SLIPKNOT
Roadrunner RR 8655-8
(digipack and standard versions);
June 1999

SLIPKNOT
Roadrunner RR 8655-8
(reissue with different tracks);
December 1999

IOWA
Roadrunner RR 12085642
August 2001

LPs

SLIPKNOT
Roadrunner RR 8655-6
(picture disc reissue, 5000 copies);
August 2000

IOWA
Roadrunner RR 12085641
(double LP)
August 2001

COMPILATION APPEARANCES

SCREAM 3
Soundtrack
(Epic, featured 'Eyeless', 2000)

KERRANG!
Spirit Of Independence
(independent, featured 'Eyeless', 2000)

DOWNLOAD 2
(Roadrunner, featured 'Surfacing (Rough Mix)', 2000)

FREE AIR FESTIVAL
Volume 2
(Go Big! Records, featured 'Wait And Bleed', 2000)

THE HARD AND THE HEAVY
Volume 2
(Redline, featured 'Spit It Out', 2000)

SWEATING BULLETS
(independent, featured 'Wait And Bleed', 2000)

MTV:
Return Of The Rock
(Roadrunner, featured 'Spit It Out', 2000)

TATTOO THE EARTH:
First Crusade
(1500 Records, features 'Surfacing (Live)' and
'Liberate (Live)', 2000)

COLLABORATIONS

SOULFLY:
Back To The Primitive
(Roadrunner, Corey appears on 'Jumpdafuckup', 2000)

VARIOUS ARTISTS: Strait Up
(Virgin, Corey appears on 'Requiem', 2000)

OFFICIAL SLIPKNOT SITES:

www.slipknot1.com

www.slipknot2.com

ROADRUNNER SITE:

www.roadrun.com

OFFICIAL PAINFACE SITE:

www.painface.com

OFFICIAL UNDONE SITE:

www.undone1.com

SR AUDIO SITE:

www.sraudio.com

KKDM SITE:

www.kkdm.com

IOWA INFORMATION:

www.iowa-counties.com/iowa

DES MOINES INFORMATION:

http://encarta.msn.com/find/
Concise.asp?z=1&pg=2&ti=761560868

DES MOINES REGISTER SITE:

www.dmregister.com

AXIOM PIERCING HOMEPAGE:

www.axiompiercing.com

ADRIAN PERTOUT'S HOMEPAGE:

www.users.bigpond.com/apertout

RAGE: THE APOCALYPSE INFORMATION:

www.shevill.freeserve.co.uk/RageTCG.html

FAN SITES:

http://members.tripod.com/
~XxNitronxX/SlipKnoT.html

www.asianet.co.jp/soze16.html

http://listen.to/slipknot

http://members.tripod.com/zzcrowzz/

http://slipknotufs.com/faq.htm

www.mfkr1.com

www.mfkr.net

www.slipknotweb.com/articles/index.phtml

http://sicfuc.cjb.net

www.geocities.com/misthunter2/slipknot

http://megapage.de/slipknot

www.expage.com/page/Slipknot67546

www.angelfire.com/ia/slipknet

NEWSGROUP:

alt.music.slipknot

OTHER SLIPKNOT INFORMATION CAN BE FOUND AT THE FOLLOWING EXCELLENT WEBSITES:

www.metalupdate.com

www.bandindex.com

www.nme.com

www.ign.com

www.sweetsuffering

www.loudside.com

www.loudandheavy.com.au

www.seattlesquare.com

★ For more information on this genre of music the reader is respectfully directed to my book on the subject, *Extreme Metal* (2000), also published by Omnibus Press.